CONTEMPORARY ISSUES
IN POLITICAL THEORY

CONTEMPORARY ISSUES IN POLITICAL THEORY

Revised Edition

Robert Booth Fowler
Jeffrey R. Orenstein

PRAEGER

New York
Westport, Connecticut
London

Library of Congress Cataloging in Publication Data

Fowler, Robert Booth, 1940-
  Contemporary issues in political theory.

  Bibliography: p.
  Includes index.
  1. Political science. I. Orenstein, Jeffrey R.
II. Title.
JA66.F65   1985   320'.01'1   84-26280
ISBN 0-275-90102-5
ISBN 0-275-91642-1 (pbk.)

Library of Congress Catalog Card Number: 84-26280
ISBN: 0-275-91642-1

First published in 1985

Praeger Publishers, One Madison Avenue, New York, NY 10010
A division of Greenwood Press, Inc.

Printed in the United States of America

The paper used in this book complies with the Permanent
Paper Standard issued by the National Information Standards
Organization (Z39.48-1984).

10 9 8 7 6 5 4 3

Preface to the Revised Edition

Political theory has continued to move in the direction of commitment and policy evaluation and prescription in the turbulent eight years that have passed since the first edition of this book. While these have been troubled times, political activism has ironically waned, at least in American culture. Today's college student remains relatively apolitical, compared to those in the early 1970s and late 1960s, and so does today's working and professional adult. Both groups display more cynicism toward politics than ever before and both groups find themselves searching for "new ideas" and ways out of the present policy malaise. It is not that today's problems are being ignored; they are merely being given lower priority than making money or personal development, perhaps to escape from political problems.

Given these trends, it is not surprising that political theorists have become a bit more aggressive in coming out of the closet of historical studies and urging people to grapple with moral issues in politics, especially such key issues as legitimacy, liberty, equality, justice, obligation, and revolt. Political theory can never be a simple or direct guide to policy making or policy makers. It cannot pretend to supply all the detailed answers to our policy questions. It can, however, supply perspective, vision, and a strong ethical voice from the wilderness that "speaks truth to power," to quote a Quaker phrase. That is why political theorists are taking strong positions on the enterprise, recognizing its obligations to speak truth, or at least to pursue it with rigor and integrity.

Political theorists have a set of skills and specialized knowledge about politics and government that can be useful in the world of who gets what, when, how. As morally engaged activists, they also have a keen interest in and often a thorough enjoyment of a good political battle joined. Thus, political theory is once again becoming committed to useful prescriptions about pressing policy problems in real political communities. Dating back almost 26 centuries to classical Athens, our tradition has entered the arena of political controversy and prescription many, many times before now, with effects ranging from the insignificant to the monumental. After all, most of our present governmental arrangements and positions on rights of citizens, for example, originated with political theorists and have been modified after the fact by statesmen and historical events. Historical studies and philosophical investigations for their own sake will always have an honored place in our intellectual arsenal and traditions, but speaking truth to power has an allure that the authors of this work applaud and join.

We are writing this revised edition, as we did the original, in the hope that you will use it as a key to unlock the door to the ever-critical moral dimensions of public life. Whether you ultimately become a policy maker or "merely" an active and thoughtful citizen, we hope that the terms, concepts, and insights contained in these pages will remain with you. We also hope that you feel the obligation with us to understand the world politically and to use your knowledge of political theory to make your own corner a better place to live for you and your neighbors.

We wish to thank the staff of Praeger for their assistance in the preparation of this edition, and a special debt is acknowledged to Joan Manahan and her staff of the Kent State University Stark Campus stenographic pool for their cheerful, accurate, and swift assistance in the physical preparation of the manuscript, above and beyond that normally expected of typists.

Contents

Freedom and Equality

CONTEMPORARY ISSUES
IN POLITICAL THEORY

1
Introduction

Political theory concerns the search for moral truth in politics. It considers what ought to exist in political life. It asks, for example, What is justice? When are we obligated to the government? When is it legitimate? What is liberty and how can we balance specific liberties and equality in political and social life? What is a good government? Is it a democracy and if so, what kind of democracy is best? This book will focus on several specific topics central to contemporary political theory: justice, liberty, democracy, and obligation.

Political theory is an exciting and important activity—exciting for the same reason it is important. It brings us face-to-face with some of the most important questions in life, especially our relations with other citizens. It challenges us to understand how other people have thought about these questions and asks us to be active participants, rather than passive spectators, by undertaking to formulate and defend our own answers to the serious and stimulating dilemmas posed in political theory.

This chapter provides a brief introduction to political theory itself. It is scarcely possible to study—much less practice—political theory without defining what political theory does and does not encompass. We also need an understanding of how political theory is normally practiced and what standards we use to distinguish good political theory from bad. Finally, we must have some idea of how people may and do justify political values.

THE NATURE OF POLITICAL THEORY

Political theory is a special form of discourse, a conversation between thoughtful people who seek to learn and communicate what is right in a moral sense in politics. Like all forms of theory, it involves the search for truth, but this does not necessarily mean an odyssey toward immutable laws or universal norms. For some thinkers it may do so, but for others the truths will be less certain and far more tentative. Perhaps political theory can provide many in our skeptical age with no more than limited insights, or intimations of partial truths and clouded suns, but the search for truth is the essential task of political theory. This quest is also, in our view, necessarily ethical. The truth we seek is how humans should behave and judge in political life. The quest is, inescapably, for moral guidance.

Sometimes political theory is termed "normative," since it is directed toward discovering norms by which we should live. Yet we do not devote our efforts exclusively to explicating normative positions on the subject of liberty and justice and the like. While we do make normative arguments, there are other important problems that concern us as students of political theory.

Political theory involves not only the formulation of a moral position in politics, but also a logical or analytic consideration of political concepts. This reflection on such basic concepts as equality and obligation is vital, because they are the foundation blocks for every political theory. To construct an argument in political theory about the nature and significance of justice, we must reflect on the alternative meanings of justice, what the word suggests, what it implies. We do this in the case of every key concept we use in the following chapters. We discuss concepts like liberty and equality in everyday language—what they seem to mean to us, as well as how they have been comprehended and explained by other political thinkers, past and present.

In addition to our discussion of basic concepts, we present and analyze alternative resolutions to the problems we treat. We do this to acquaint the student with the main views on such subjects as the proper stance regarding justice or obligation, and because political theory necessarily involves this kind of analysis. Only by knowing and arguing about alternative perspectives can we strengthen our own argument and communicate with others who hold differing viewpoints. Only by analysis can we assure ourselves that we have considered opposing views, taken them seriously, and honestly endeavored to garner whatever fruits they may offer. When we discuss political obligation, for instance, we eventually argue normatively, trying to defend a certain view of obligation and its implications in the political sphere. We do so, however, only after a careful analytical investigation of possible alternatives.

No matter how thoroughly we pursue the three main aspects of political theory—reflection on basic concepts, analysis of alternative views, and the pursuit of normative truth—we must remember that political theory is unique as a philosophical subject, because it is conducted in a political context. There is no easy definition of politics; it is a complicated yet fascinating enterprise. We simply suggest that politics encompasses conflicts and agreements in the public realm. It is this public aspect that is the crucial defining feature, one that distinguishes politics (however imperfectly) from those areas of life that we all consider more immediately private, personal, and limited. Thus political theory includes questions of justice, because justice concerns the proper relations among people in such obviously public arenas as the law or the distribution of economic goods. It includes political obligation, because this is a relationship among citizens. But it rarely includes the relations between a brother and a sister or between lovers or between a man and his flower garden or a woman and her hobby.

What Political Theory Is Not

We do not pretend that our concept of political theory is the only possible one, though it is not uncommon. It is, however, a view that excludes certain types of activity. Thus we must clarify what we do not consider political theory. In particular, political theory is not the same as the following types of activity that are sometimes confused with it: ordinary opinion, personal feelings, ideology, practical politics, policy judgments, history, and political science.

Political theory is not ordinary opinion because, unlike opinion, it can be sustained only by reasoned analysis and justification. To have an opinion on justice or liberty is not the same thing as consideration of the concept of justice, analysis of alternative visions of justice, and careful argument for the truth of one vision. Opinion is usually casual and lacks mature reflection and justification. In this sense we do not believe that most people are ordinarily political philosophers, even though they may have opinions about justice, equality, and many other matters in politics.

Even more, political theory is not the same thing as the expression of individual feelings. It may well be true that all our political theories are rooted in the first place, and maybe in the last place, in our feelings, as psychologists might contend. But stating a position on justice by saying "I feel" this or that is not political theory. Nor is defending a view on obligation by asserting "Well, I just feel obligated" much of an argument in political theory. What these I-feel statements are, of course, are merely reports on one's psychological dispositions. We all have them and we all draw on them, but reasoned arguments about what ought to be in politics they are not.

On the other hand, we do not think political theory can be equated with ideology—world views are all-encompassing, held to be absolutely true and highly action oriented. Political theory is just not about propounding total visions. It involves, instead, intellectual search, reflection, argument, and painstaking enlightenment. It is not about a place to rest, a surrender of the mind to simple faith, but an invitation to thought, to communication, to argument. It is not the realm of dogmatists, but of thinkers and arguers.

Nor is political theory about a rush to action. It is not unrelated to action, but it should not be a substitute for action. For many of us, in fact, its largest purpose is to obtain guidance for action as citizens in politics. This is not its only function, however, since understanding what is right in politics is a good in itself. None of us can expect whatever political values we are able to develop to be easily translated into specific recommendations for particular circumstances or immediate policy choices. The purpose of political theory is to examine the nature of broader concepts, such as liberty and democracy, rather than to give policy makers specific answers for proper decisions. A thorough grounding in the principles of political theory surely can illuminate many policy choices in politics, but it cannot do more. There is a considerable distance between the general and the specific, a reality that sometimes annoys those who want political theory to provide quick policy advice. This reaction is understandable, but so is the reaction of many political theorists who complain that the people who are entirely policy oriented do not look to the broader normative context and the wider realm of principle without which their policy decisions lack needed perspective.

Political theory should also be distinguished from history, although so often it is not. We respect the history of political philosophy, but we do not think it is a substitute for the ongoing process of new thinking. It is for just this reason that we have chosen to follow an approach in this book that concentrates on political theory as a living analytical and normative process, rather than a study of great thinkers of the past. The historical approach, the process of reducing political theory from an active enterprise to a review of what others in the past have taught, often diverts us from molding our own political theory. It can transform us into passive observers of the work and times of Hobbes or Marx, but does not enable us to craft any political theory for ourselves.

Moreover, an exclusively retrospective focus often ignores the fact that all our exemplars in this activity need not be historical. Political theory, often of a high order, occurs today as well as yesterday (and presumably always will). The writings of John Rawls, Michael Walzer, Milton Friedman, and Daniel Bell constitute recent outstanding examples.

The great tradition of Western thought, the inevitable background of contemporary political theory, may be viewed in several ways, all valuable for us. This tradition, spanning the centuries from the Greeks of ancient Athens to great nineteenth-century thinkers such as Mill, Marx, and Freud, forms a body of thought that is valuable on its own. Its investigation can be—and for us often is—a voyage into the history of particular eras and places, a way to expand and sensitize our minds, as well as an aesthetic pleasure. In the context of this book, however, we see it as primarily a resource. This resource constitutes a debate between people—both men and women—as concerned in the past as we are in the present with enduring (if not always identical) problems of political morality—from justice to political obligation to liberty. We dare not ignore this vast historical treasury in studying contemporary political theory, any more than we should make the exploration of its riches a substitute for our own efforts in political theory.

Finally, political theory is not identical (although it may at times be congruent) with most of what we think of today as political science. There is no universal agreement on the points of difference, but two are usually noted. The first concerns the contrasting goals of most modern political theorists and political scientists. We know political theorists are mainly concerned to discover truth about how people should live together in political communities. The fundamental focus is ethical and not necessarily factual. It concentrates on what is morally right rather than on facts or theories about how people actually behave at this time. At its core is the task of value judgment and argument. Political science, however, seeks to discover how men and women act in political life, sometimes attempting to formulate, insofar as possible, laws that may govern political behavior. In this process, most political scientists, while acknowledging the challenge of the task, undertake to keep their work as free as possible from normative judgments.

Second, political science and political theory often pursue different methods. Political scientists do propose theories, but they are theories of the operation of the "real" world. Then they undertake to test their theories or hypotheses by gathering factual information that sustains or undermines their theories. The crucial test for them is scientific: the correspondence of their empirical theories with the world of fact or, in an alternative conception, their nonfalsifiability by empirical data. Political theory, in contrast, does not attempt to prove empirical theories, or to use empirical information only. Its characteristic mode of procedure is to argue for one moral position or another by rational means, calling on linguistic, utilitarian, and often deductive (from first principles found in nature, the divine, the human person, or history) arguments. Empirical data are not ignored, but they constitute only one factor in a search for the best ethical argument.

It is the first difference that is probably the crucial one. Political science is usually a contrasting activity to political theory, because political science like all science, searches for the truths that describe how things actually are, while political theory focuses on how they ought to be. Neither activity is superior to the other. Both are demanding, worthwhile tasks, yet they should not be confused. It is one thing to describe how Congress operates or to formulate a theory about how democratic legislatures function and test it with facts drawn from the actual practice of contemporary democratic legislatures, and another to argue how democratic legislatures should operate or whether we should have democratic government at all.

Political science and political theory often overlap. For example, political theories usually contain empirical claims or assertions, since arguments about what ought to be in politics normally involve considerations about what is possible in the real world. And one of the great weaknesses of many political theories is that such empirical claims do not always receive a rigorous defense in terms of the canons of scientific activity. Political writings often abound in statements about human nature or behavior, about how political systems operate, or regarding what is possible—without a factual basis beyond the illusions of personal intuition or common sense. This is never acceptable, One must argue both empirical and normative claims.

Political Theory, Good and Bad

There are no inflexible guidelines that denote what good political theory is, but there are some well-understood principles that most practitioners invoke to characterize it. We think four are particularly significant and worthy of mention, in order to assist you in assessing our arguments to follow—and your own efforts.

First, we must know as clearly as possible what are the basic values (or the fundamental premises) that underlie any argument in political theory. Time and again arguments are undermined by vague or ambiguous basic premises. This failure to make clear the underlying norms can easily be a fatal mistake. Thus before one begins to defend one theory or another of justice or obligation, it is essential to make clear just what one wants in terms of justice and why, or just what one seeks through obligation and why. These are the vital first principles that guide everyone turning to political issues in political theory, and without them one's arguments are inevitably adrift. In the process it is not enough to state "where one is coming from." It is essential to defend this starting point, turning it over aloud or on paper until it emerges as a richly explored and defended beginning perspective.

Second, good political theory requires that basic rules of deduction, logic, and consistency be followed. Very often normative arguments in politics are grounded in deductions from first premises that do not really follow logically. A classic example is the argument that liberal democracy is the appropriate form of government, once we realize that there are no ultimate truths for politics. The argument goes like this: Assuming there are no absolute answers, it is logical to deduce that tolerance is a vital value, since we would not want to close off any choices. Then, agreeing that tolerance is what we want to encourage, it follows that liberal democracy is the most appropriate political system, since it is the most committed to tolerance. This is a much less logical view than it at first seems. There is no necessary logic to the idea that if there are no answers, we should therefore support tolerance; we might or we might not. Futhermore, even if we endorse tolerance, it will not necessarily follow that liberal democracy (majority rule and minority rights) will give us the most tolerance; this would be a matter for empirical investigation.

Consistency is important, too—consistency in continuing to base an argument on the same fundamental value(s) and not assuming one at the beginning of an argument and quite another at the end—consistency, as well, in using key words and concepts in the same way throughout an entire argument. For example, it is hard to take seriously an argument about liberty that alters the meaning of liberty six or seven times during its course. Nothing seems more obvious, and yet it is not always easy to avoid this common and dangerous pitfall.

Third, in addition to the importance of being clear about basic values and their justification and seeking to be consistent and logical, a satisfactory political theory must demonstrate a good deal of breadth. It must cast a wide net of argumentation, incorporating many sides and views of a problem into its own treatment of a subject. In treating justice, for instance, it should show awareness of how justice is talked about in the present time and how it has been considered in classic formulations of the past. It must not ignore the dilemmas and possible pitfalls without which no sophistication can be developed. Indeed, it should properly examine its own formulations against others. Far too often practitioners of political theory do not ask themselves what objections others would have to their view. This not only diminishes the appeal that any argument can make to others who may have differing perspectives; it also deprives political theorists of the gains that result from a rigorous challenge to their viewpoint. Positions and values are not self-evident; they have to be defended; and fortunately, in the defense they either get better or they fall. Without challenge they are untested and vulnerable.

Finally, good political theory must provide insight into the problem it tackles. Great political theorists like Plato and Hobbes are admired because what they had to say about politics and human life provides precious insight even now. What is unique about many of the greatest thinkers in the long tradition of political thought is that they were able to look at familiar problems (such as liberty, obligation, or justice) and see them in rather original ways, casting a new light that was creative and educational. This is the most basic requirement of all—and the most challenging.

JUSTIFICATION OF POLITICAL VALUES

Many people tend to assume that their moral positions are eminently reasonable and that many of the objections to them are ridiculous. Yet, at the same time, when they are pressed to defend their political values, they often take refuge in relativism, declaring that their values are fine for them and others' are fine for others. Neither the assumption of the self-evidence of our perspectives, however, nor assertions of value relativism do anything to meet a crucial standard for a satisfactory political theory—the need for a clear and thoughtful justification of basic values.

Sooner or later every political argument comes to rest on basic norms and the justification for them. This is inevitable and we cannot ignore it. Thus every political theory must take account of its first principles and the frameworks in which they are developed and defended.

The painful truth is that dealing with the foundations of any political theory is demanding. We have all been involved in discussions or arguments that came to a dead end because the two sides ultimately realized that their fundamental starting points seemed neither arguable nor reconcilable. We cannot overcome this problem in this book. We are concerned with specific political values, not how they might be ultimately justified. And we know as well as anybody else that disagreements about fundamentals are not easy to overcome. It is essential, however, to begin a book on political theory by granting that justifications do differ, identifying what the main justifications are, and emphasizing that awareness of one's fundamental perspective is essential in constructing and defending any political position.

Ethical Relativism

Political theorists have employed four types of justification, some of which have important subdivisions. None is more popular today than ethical relativism. Proponents of this view deny that there are any absolute truths relevant to politics and political choice. They insist that the only justification for values in politics is personal preference. They urge people to admit this reality, that subjective feelings govern moral choices and nothing else really can, and to avoid pretending that there are fancier or more pretentious grounds for political norms. As they see it, relativism has two prime advantages. It teaches us that no one should be too quick or too confident in proclaiming what others ought to believe or do. After all, they say, we all have our own ideas and it is hard to show that one person is closer to the truth than anyone else. Second, they maintain that once people learn to get along with the reality of ethical relativism, it will provide them a grounding for their values—all anyone needs, as long as we practice some tolerance for others.

A famous version of ethical relativism is the emotive theory of ethics developed by A. J. Ayer. It holds that political theory has its roots in individual feelings. Arguments about what is right in politics are really little more than expressions of different personal feelings—hence, the label some have applied to ethical and political arguments, calling them boo-hurrah arguments. No matter how elegant the argument, what is really going on is boos or hurrahs on the basis of individual emotive reactions. For some analysts this fact is a sad one, since it seems to imply that reason does not play much of a role in political theory; others are not so pessimistic, contending that we can reason a good deal over political norms as long as we remember that in the end we have no final justification except our feelings. They believe the real danger comes from people who do not understand themselves well enough to realize that their values are grounded in subjective sentiments and who tend to talk of absolute truths. They fear that people can too easily move from talk to action, imposing their subjective wills on others in the name of grand absolutes that are no more than individuals' personal feelings.

Another version of ethical relativism talks less about feelings and concentrates more on experiences. According to this outlook, our political values express our particular experiences in life, the habits we form, and the customs we learn. They can be expressed in rational terms, and they should be, but all rational justifications are more or less rationalizations for our individual experiences. This analysis also asserts there are no absolute truths, only particular experiences, and defends the consequent necessity for tolerance if we are to live together.

The Existentialist Justification

A second form of justification is the existentialist position. Existentialists view the relation between individuals and their world as absurd, not only without absolute meaning but also without any meaning. They believe it is preposterous to think that any political values can be justified in absolute terms. What the individual is left with is the stark reality of a life often filled with pain and guaranteed only to end in death. We have, so to say, our existence, but no truths, no essences, to guide us. Existentialists believe that what we must do in these circumstances is choose values to follow in life, including political norms. They urge that we choose as thoughtfully and as rationally as possible, but choose with a clear-headed understanding that we can never be certain of the correct answer. The problem they see is that many choose, in Jean Paul Sartre's phrase, in "bad faith." They choose political norms that they hope will allow them to choose no more and avoid the responsibility that choice entails, that will allow them to escape the inescapable reality that there is no absolute answer and no avoidance of responsibility. People cling to political ideologies and totalitarian hopes, rather than courageously going on day after day, choosing as situations arise. The existentialist test, then, for an adequate justification of a political norm is twofold: Is the norm self-consciously chosen, and do its consequences affirm us as choosing human beings, responsible for those consequences?

Absolutism

A third group of justifications often employed in political philosophy follows quite another direction. It maintains that political values must have and can have absolute justifications. One form is the eternally attractive and popular natural-law argument that holds that one or more political values are absolutely true for all times, places, and people. Sometimes natural-law arguments take the form of asserting that there are certain duties or laws that apply to all of us. This was the position of the classic natural lawyer, St. Thomas Aquinas. He contended that God set down certain norms that were permanently binding and that must always be obeyed to the best of fallible human ability. Another form is rather more familiar to Americans—the natural-rights argument. This viewpoint declares that there are certain rights, such as life or liberty, that are guaranteed by nature (or God through nature) to all people forever. It becomes the duty of governments to protect and to realize these rights. The classic expression of this position is in our own Declaration of Independence. A third variety that is widespread among a number of contemporary thinkers claims that there are certain basic needs that we all have as human beings. Its advocates insist that it is a matter of absolute right that they be fulfilled.

Other forms of justification that are absolute in their character include those that draw on history. There is the Marxist justification, that the dialectical processes of history provide the essential justification for what is right in politics. Consider Marx's views on the capitalist order as an example. Marx is often erroneously interpreted as believing that capitalism is an unmitigated evil. In fact, Marx believed that when history brought capitalism to a nation, it was a good thing. On the other hand, when historical processes brought capitalism toward its demise, as they inevitably did, then capitalism was no longer a good, no longer annointed by history.

Another version of the historical justification that is also influential today is the conservative argument from tradition. Many conservatives explicitly or implicitly make past history, or a certain version of it, into an absolute value that manifests the culmination of human wisdom and that ought not to be transgressed.

Other Justifications

A final set of justifications try, sometimes awkwardly, to steer between relativist and absolutist positions. These include pragmatism, utilitarianism, and dependence on the wisdom of experts. Pragmatists maintain that the test of political values ought to be their concrete worth in practice in speaking to situational human needs. Though this approach is common in the United States, it is a weak justification in its more ordinary form, for to justify something on its practicality involves the assumption that X is practical for achieving Z without telling us why it is that we want to get to Z. That is, it does not really provide us with any basis for our ultimate values.

Much more satisfactory is the utilitarian justification. Utilitarianism suggests that values are sound if they promote the greatest good for the greatest number or advance the general public interest or happiness. Such a view does skate between an absolute-value position and sheer relativism. To be sure, it is not always easy to measure the greatest good for the greatest number, or to assess happiness. Moreover, terms like "public interest" are notoriously hard to define. This view does, however, take seriously individual desires and interests, while seeking an overall public good.

Another variety, proposed by T. D. Weldon in his classic *The Vocabulary of Politics*, suggests that we think about justification in political theory the way art critics think about art. His idea is that art and political theory share a common dilemma in that neither can have recourse to verifiable absolute standards, yet this does not prevent the world of art from reaching broad agreement on which paintings are great. There are well-known and widely shared norms for good art that are upheld and developed by those who are most experienced in the study of art—art critics. He proposes that political critics—those who know the most about politics and political theory—ought to be the judges of what is a good political theory and what is not.

No matter which of the many justifications one finds appealing, a good political theory must have one laid on the table, so that its starting place is clear. There is no doubt that arguing about final justifications is much harder than arguing over such political values as democracy or justice, yet at the least one's starting point must be indicated. Without it no political theory is complete.

SUGGESTIONS FOR SUPPLEMENTARY READING

Anderson, Charles W. *Statecraft: An Introduction to Political Choice and Judgment.* New York: Wiley, 1977.

Barry, Brian. *Political Argument.* New York: Humanities Press, 1965.

Germino, Dante. *Beyond Ideology: The Revival of Political Theory.* New York: Harper & Row, 1967.

Hanson, Donald W. "The Nature of Political Philosophy." vii–xx In *Obligation and Dissent,* edited by D. Hanson and R. B. Fowler, Boston: Little, Brown, 1971.

Murphy, Joseph S. *Political Theory: A Conceptual Analysis.* Homewood, Ill.: Dorsey Press, 1968.

Oppenheim, Felix. *Moral Principles in Political Philosophy.* New York: Random House, 1968.

Sabine, George. *A History of Political Theory.* New York: Holt, Rinehart and Winston, 1961.

Sibley, Mulford Q. *Political Ideas and Ideologies.* New York: Harper & Row, 1970.

Spitz, David (Ed.). *Political Theory and Social Change.* New York: Atherton, 1967.

Tinder, Glenn. *Political Thinking: The Perennial Questions.* Boston: Little, Brown, 1974.

Toulmin, Stephen. *Reason in Ethics.* Cambridge: Cambridge University Press, 1968.

Weldon, T. D. *The Vocabulary of Politics.* Baltimore, Md. Penguin Books, 1953.

Wolfe, Alan, and Charles McCoy. *Political Analysis: An Unorthodox Approach.* New York: Crowell, 1972.

2
Politics, Democracy, and Their Critics

As the twentieth century wanes, democracy has a strong grip on the collective imaginations of statesmen and thinkers. Virtually all of the nations and movements of the world profess to be democratic in one form or another, often with "unique" variations. When heads of state of seven Western nations met in London in 1984 for their tenth annual economic summit conference, they felt compelled not only to deal with economic issues, but to issue a statement of "democratic principles." Although the statement itself was even less memorable than most of a similar nature issued by politicians who are not practicing political theorists, it joined a long train of attempts by statesmen, dating back to Pericles, to define democracy and associate themselves with it.

This chapter focuses on what democrats share, what the case for democracy is, and the views of critics of democracy. It also focuses on the preliminary questions of the legitimacy of politics and government in general, because these are thresholds of the critical issues of democracy, and none of these questions can be separated, either in principle or in practice. Surely, if politics is not a worthy activity, it is pointless to evaluate the best kind of government and to assess the claims and counterclaims of democratic proponents and opponents.

That the value of politics is under attack is familiar to contemporary Americans, after decades of divisive foreign policy and scandals in leadership morality, but the problem is not a uniquely American one. Revolutions, terrorist attacks, and demonstrations around the world, from the Sikh rebellion in India to the protests in the Philippines, indicate the seemingly universal mood of dissatisfaction with governments and politics as usual. The fallout from Watergate and Abscam, scandals like Cervaso in Europe, and the failure of public officials to fulfill earlier lofty promises in nations that recently threw off the yoke of colonialism stimulate widespread disgust with politicians and politics. This is a finding substantiated by our neighbors, as well as public opinion polls, low voter turnouts, and support for rebels in various parts of the world.

There is nothing inevitable about these sentiments. British public opinion, for example, has a very high regard for its political processes and personalities, in spite of Britain's weighty political problems. There is evidence that Americans, in particular, have held politics in low esteem for a long time. We should note, however, that throughout history there have always been people, from Aristotle to Jefferson to Camus, who have affirmed the validity and utility of political communities, denying that politics is necessarily unsavory, corrupt, or boring. The debate is between those thinkers who doubt the worth of politics and those who either view it as a necessary if limited good or place great hope in political activity, seeing it as one of the most glorious human endeavors. It is one of the most significant public questions humanity must face.

A second basic question, flowing logically out of the first, is whether we ought to have a political community at all—especially a government, which is a highly organized political community. Politics may have its uses, may even be a natural attribute of people, but do we need to have a state? This may appear to be a strange question, because all societies we know have governments and we are well socialized to think the existence of governments justified. The question needs to be investigated in detail before we embrace a form of government like democracy. All of us have at least a trace of the anarchist in our souls in the resentment we harbor toward the state at tax time, or when we are thwarted by laws we think are stupid, or when we consider the vast sums of money squandered by military establishments. The history of political thought contains many anarchists whose utter contempt for the immorality of government in theory and practice has led them to press for the destruction of the state, although not necessarily of politics.

Ultimately, we suggest that politics and even organized governments have a great deal of utility, although anarchists have many telling points that cannot be ignored. This becomes apparent when we consider the interrelated questions of the nature of the best kind of state, of who should rule, and by what authority. The present, like the past, abounds in an almost infinite variety of ideals of government and sets of rulers, each loudly claiming legitimate authority. Dictators, oligarchies of the rich, military juntas, Marxists, and other more or less democratic systems all proclaim themselves to be the embodiment of legitimacy. We conclude that only governments that are firmly democratic in practice as well as rhetoric, those resting on popular participation and responsiveness, may validly make this claim. It should be made clear from the outset, however, that there is no need to commit ourselves to the orthodox Western idea of representative democracy. Democracy is considerably broader than the U.S. and British versions.

This leads to the final concern of this chapter: What are the fundamentals of democracy that we can agree upon? Our age, as any other, still hears the charge by critics of democracy (admitted or not) that the major existing "democratic" states are merely hollow images of "true" democracy. Using the insights of both the anarchists and democratic as well as antidemocratic statists, we ask what democracy really is and pave the way for the examination in the next chapter of what form is best. These are basic questions, because they cut to the heart of the justification and character of the states that we all live with. They are so basic that they must be thoroughly considered before we can move to more complex values like justice, liberty, equality, obligation, and revolt, all of which are based on perspectives of these foundations.

POLITICS

What is politics? Is it a valuable human activity? Can it be dispensed with? Should it be? Clearly, it is not perfectly obvious that politics is critically important. To be sure, many citizens from the most ordinary people of today to the great religious prophets of yesterday have not thought that it was. Most political science students, public officials, and political philosophers, however, take it for granted that politics deserves our interest and participation. How do we decide who is right?

There is no single or simple definition of politics, but as our introductory discussion makes evident, we see politics as a broad set of relationships concerned with the public integration of human needs and possibilities. It involves conflict and consensus in the public realm over who gets what, when, how, and why. It is about what roads are built, what TV stations are licensed, who supplies our electricity with what type of fuel at what cost, both in dollars and in environmental quality, and what politicians are elected, if any. It is also about things other than the scramble for tax dollars, welfare subsidies, and elections. It involves such moral questions as the appropriateness of pornography, TV violence, or gun control; spiritual and religious matters, such as the relationship between church and state; and symbolic questions, such as the treatment of the flag or the observance of public holidays. In the final analysis it is the inescapable relationships in the public sphere of people who share the earth together, who have to come to terms with each other in one way or another. Politics, for better or for worse, concerns both the problems and prospects of people who have no choice but to deal with each other by war, love, or anything in between. It is not defined by manipulations and power any more than it is defined by justice and equality, but surely it involves all of them sooner or later.

Since there are many opinions about the relative value of politics, there are many sides to this eternal debate. Four views particularly merit our attention: that politics is of limited use for society as a whole, that it is of use for merely personal needs, that it is the highest human enterprise, and that it lacks any kind of genuine value.

Politics as Limitedly Useful

The viewpoint that politics has uses for society, but only if its range of concerns and demands is carefully delimited, is by all indications the ordinary perspective of most Americans. This is a long-popular viewpoint, first articulated in an undeveloped manner in ancient Greece,[1] holding that people inevitably form groups and seek to gain their own—and hopefully general—benefit from public activity. Some modern proponents insist politics is especially necessary today, because we coexist in large, complex, and expanding social orders that contain great possibilities of social conflict. They feel that politics may assist us as we try to live together with a minimum of conflict and a maximum of cooperative and fair dealing. Consequently, they contend, that it is wise to accept some politics in order to get what limited help we can from it.

Advocates of the limited-use theory of politics repeatedly stipulate that politics can never be more than a tool for societies and individuals. Just as it is foolish to pretend that we can do without politics, so it is dangerous to make politics an end in itself. For most Americans and to a somewhat lesser extent for Europeans, for example, politics takes a back seat to private personal or business activities in what people view as salient concerns. In polities like the People's Republic of China of the 1980s, however, this is less true. In much of the developing world, political institutions not only carry a heavy load of economic development tasks but also enjoy much more public attention (both positive and negative).

The fact is that many people feel that the sinful or selfish nature of people determines human behavior substantially more than does politics. Thus, politics simply cannot be a very significant enterprise. Reinhold Niebuhr, a great American religious and political thinker of the twentieth century, developed this perspective. He argued that too much involvement and faith in politics can easily lead to political fanaticism, concentration camps, and the murder of millions. Those who become too devoted to political life can lose perspective and make serious moral misjudgments of what politics and government can accomplish in this world of sin, habit, and popular apathy. They may try to force people to adhere to a particular vision of the good society at great social cost. Niebuhr also argued, along with many others who wish to acknowledge the value of politics while stressing its limits, that politics should not be confused with features of life that are not means but the ends that constitute what is truly worthwhile in human experience. Politics should not be confused with life itself, with God, with love and joy, nor with family and friends. Against them, politics is secondary.[2]

This mostly negative view of politics, reinforced by constant media spotlighting of government waste, crass motives of politicians, and public fraud and inefficiency (while generally ignoring government efficiencies, honesties, and everyday successfully cost-effective provision of necessary services) has some important negative consequences. It has to be a major contributor to the lack of interest many talented young people show in political careers, just as their talented parents have done. It also certainly has an effect on the failure of many school and local tax levies, which are turned down by voters who feel governments just waste money instead of producing useful services. Critically, the United States has the lowest voter turnout and political participation level of all the industrial "democracies" in the world. Surely, the low esteem politics has in our culture has a causal impact on this. It is a self-fulfilling prophecy—and it has its costs.

Politics as Fulfilling Personal Needs

Another image of politics sees political life as a justifiable activity only insofar as it fulfills one's personal need for fun, excitement, or power. Sometimes, as Harold Lasswell argued a generation ago, it may even be the vehicle for displacement of dangerous neurotic private needs and compulsions from the dark side of our souls.[3] In one way or another, however, this is the dominant political disposition of many actual and would-be officeholders and politicans. It is an attitude that grips endless student interns in state capitals and in Washington. It is the driving energy of many of the young and the not so young who participate in political campaigns by licking envelopes, canvassing, giving advice, or even donating money. Not all interns are there for these reasons, nor does this activate all party workers and politicians, but anyone who has worked in any of these capacities knows how many of those involved in politics have little vision of its broad public value, but a keen appreciation of its personal value to them.

This approach to politics is probably harmless enough, unless it is held by many people with great power. That would raise serious questions. The objective of politics might then become merely the self-satisfaction of those who participate in it, relegating more vital public ends to unimportance. Winning may then become all important, as may supporting a winner regardless of his or her views, for there is far more power and excitement in being on top in politics (or anything else) than being on the bottom. Perspective and vision of general public purpose slip away too easily in this mode.

The danger is that the politician or politico can become excessively preoccupied with one dimension of life, losing sight of any principles beyond success and political loyalty. This sort of obsessive slant on politics led straight to the abuses uncovered in the Watergate, "Debategate," and Abscam scandals, where powerful people lost concern for anything but the necessity of maintaining their personal power through political victory at any cost.

Politics as the Highest Human Enterprise

A third view of the political dimensions of life involves a commitment that goes far beyond what most people give to politics or what they respect in others who choose to do so. It asserts that politics is far more important and far nobler than is recognized by those who would limit its reach or use it merely for the satisfaction of personal needs. This perspective ranks politics as the highest human enterprise, because it claims that we must focus on how people live together and the best way to do it successfully. We cannot avoid problems in living together and thus we cannot avoid politics. In fact, we ought to dedicate ourselves to it, rather than hoping it will go away. No task could possibly be more vital to us. Consequently, no task could be more honorable or important, because our humanity is our most honorable and important possession.

The ancient Athenians celebrated the tremendous worth of politics, which is why they honored great politicians and statesmen over all men. They felt politics was the highest human activity. Many supporters of participatory democracy today also praise politics. For them direct, popular self-government through political activity is the essence of the good life. The ideal of public service among British aristocrats over the past several centuries illustrates these values. The same applies to some of America's political "aristocrats," such as the Kennedys, the Rockefellers, the Roosevelts, and the Harrimans. No one can deny their interest in the power and excitement of politics, but it would be perverse to ignore their considerable devotion to the principles of public service, often at great personal costs to health, family, and fortune.

In the period since World War II a number of political thinkers have defended this perspective. Some, like Hannah Arendt, contend that politics is so unsatisfactory today because it has forsaken the ancient Greek belief that political action is the best mechanism humans have found for personal and political growth. Others, like Albert Camus, stress their belief that only in active political communities can men and women achieve the personal dignity and social development that is the highest human ideal. All agree that our distaste for politics in its best and most responsible forms amounts to an unnecessary surrender of our own human potentials and a retreat to human privatism and selfishness that is as personally self-defeating as it is socially disastrous.[4]

The problem that this perspective faces in the contemporary West is that few really believe it. We do not perceive that politics is more important than family life or, often, religion. Clearly it plays a much smaller role in the existence of the average person than does work or family. In addition, many people observe that the ideal of public service, or even activism on issues of political morality, requires a lot of time or money. It also necessitates a good deal of energy, which few have after a long day's work in societies that make economic activity so important and public service so remote. Few except an elite of upper-middle-class or wealthy people can readily devote themselves to politics. The rest of us are too busy paying the bills. We must remember that Athens was a slave society, as well as a paradise of political activity.

Another kind of objection to this approach makes a different point. Many contemporary social scientists, most famously Bernard Berelson, warn against the uncritical celebration of the ideal of active political involvement. They say that widespread participation or commitment in politics is dangerous.

Berelson and others prefer a largely inactive or apathetic populace. They fear that mass mobilization or intense interest in politics might activate a large number of citizens who are ignorant about political issues and candidates and who bring only irrationality to the political process. Some opponents of easy access to voter participation, like former Ohio State Senator Thomas Van Meter who was quoted as saying that his party lost an election "because too many people voted," reflect this opinion. Others have noted that broad mass participation can lead swiftly to totalitarian tyrants and demagogues. They cite as a case in point the intense political atmosphere of the early 1930s in Germany, when Hitler came to power.[5]

These views claim that investing politics with great importance tends to raise absurdly inflated expectations about what it can do in alleviating human ills, or to produce sometimes dangerous disappointments when politics turns out to be unable to deliver Nirvana or Utopia. They have a point, but it is never simple to decide when the politics of promise and activism goes too far in its faith and raises too many hopes. Politics does deliver beneficial change from time to time. Some Reaganites, for example, have accused Lyndon Johnson of causing substantial psychic hurt to millions of America's poor by declaring the War on Poverty in the middle 1960s, which made extravagant claims about abolishing poverty in one generation. They ask what good was there in promising what politics could not—and did not—produce. The facts of the matter, however, show that there was real progress made in ameliorating poverty, until Reagan's massive slashes in social programs in the early 1980s stopped it and reversed the trend.

Yet it must also be pointed out that politics in some form always goes on. The apathetic may be "safe" when they remain quiescent, but we must surely realize that by acquiescence, by apathy, we always grant control over our lives to those who do believe in politics. The apathetic are never masters of their political destiny and they are all too often the victims in history. Those who celebrate apathy, or even try to explain it away as not so bad, may often be political conservatives wearing the clothes of neutral social scientists or elitist politicians who wish to maintain control.

Amid the warnings of the dangers of politics we should never forget the uses of politics. Politics and political action have produced great changes, many for the better. They produced constitutions, civil liberties, and even (for better or for worse) the modern welfare state. Politics' value must not be ignored, even as its dangers are acknowledged. Clearly, for us as human beings who share the same point in time, a common set of institutions through which we can conduct our relations in the public sphere is indispensable.

The Irrelevancy of Politics

Juxtaposed to these viewpoints, a final and enduring popular concept of politics not only denies that politics is the highest human enterprise but also argues that it is not much use at all. This is an extension of the common U.S. view of politics, although it seems perplexing to political science students and professors, not to mention politicians, who recognize the benefits political communities provide on a regular basis.

One aspect of this perspective contends that there are much more salient dimensions to life than politics, such as family, work, faith, or the rhythm of ongoing nature. Job, family, and friends occupy the central places in the life of the average person. Even watching a taped movie or game at home on TV, watering the lawn, hacking on a home computer, preparing for a daughter's wedding, or going bowling with friends attracts far more people in a day than scores of political rallies do in a year, because these many other features in life appear to be more vital to their daily existence. This, too, is a price a polity pays for distrust. The fewer who participate, the greater the impact of the minorities who exercise their clout on the policy process.

Another aspect emphasizes the paramount significance of religion over all else, very much including political activity. Such disparate religious teachers as Tolstoy, Lao Tzu, and some Christian fundamentalists teach that only religious salvation matters in the end and that we should ignore such evil concerns as politics. Others, such as some nineteenth-century anarchists or the famous behavioral psychologist of today B. F. Skinner, scorn politics because there is an earthly "way"—there is a solution to all of the problems that politics deals with so badly and at so much human cost. Whether they favor a free anarchist community or a behaviorally engineered utopia, they urge us to ignore conventional politics and concentrate on preparation for the politics-free society.[6] This attitude contrasts markedly, of course, with the recent tendency of evangelical Christian groups in the United States to become politically involved in order to protect their values, but even they argue that it is ultimately irrelevant to the Christian soul.

Finally, there are those who reject politics because it is just another trivial human activity, meaningless before the eternal verities and cycles of nature. They place politics against nature and see it as degrading in comparison with the grandeur and inspiration of nature. We think at once of Thoreau at Walden, on the Merrimac, or at Cape Cod, and relive his immortal words of celebration of the glories of a natural world he knew so well. We recall his angry words of protest over the follies and futilities of human politics,[7] as topical as the contempt for politicians often present in today's corporate boardrooms.

These antipolitical stances not only share the belief that politics is a secondary concern, they also agree on the proposition that politics is ordinarily dangerous. After all, if God, utopia, or nature is what really matters, then any interest we show in politics is ultimately a diversion of our minds and energies from what we should really care about. It is a snare and a temptation that can lead us astray into a snakepit before we know it.

The eloquence of the opponents of politics echoes throughout the history of human thought, but its force need not lead us to ignore the mundane but significant truth that there is more to life than work, nature, or even a distant utopia. There are also other people and our relationships with them. They count too, and they are indeed the very heart and marrow of a full and decent life. We must live with them as a practical matter and we hope to live well with them as an ideal. We repeat our earlier point: Politics is the way in which we can and must regulate our lives together. It is potentially a mechanism for helping each other. It can even be a means for human growth. Its operations may be imperfect or worse; yet, if we ignore it, we doubt that our inevitably collective life will improve. We are inescapably thrust into interdependence with each other. If politics is not the highest of enterprises through which we accommodate ourselves to that reality, it is scarcely the lowest.

We need it even if it is of restricted use in our complex world. The alternative is to surrender any aspiration that through public interaction we may grow together. It is also to surrender to the few who do care about politics the power to determine the public side of our existence. In an era when scientists are making new discoveries about the even more horrible than previously imagined consequences of nuclear war, it might be surrendering to the few the power over whether any of us exist at all.

STATISTS VERSUS ANARCHISTS

Recognizing the need for some politics, we must turn to one of the classic debates in the history of political ideas, that between those who defend government and the state and the anarchists who accept politics but reject the state.

Anarchists indict all forms of the state and other organized centers of power, such as the church, the multinational corporation, or the university, as we know them. For them, states are inevitably organized political communities, distinguished by governments with extensive coercive powers. They feel that states are despicable and dangerous as a result. Their denunciations raise a vexing question: Is the existence of the state and government morally defensible? We tend to take their necessity and moral appropriateness for granted, even though we may not like one or another form of them. Yet it is an error to assume that government is automatically a good idea in human affairs, without carefully evaluating anarchist ideas.

Anarchic viewpoints are not uniquely modern. In classical Athens the Cynic Diogenes took an anarchical view of the state, denied the need for it, and challenged its claims of legitimacy. While it can be found in all periods of history, anarchism had its most extensive appeal in the nineteenth century, producing such diverse spokesmen as the Russian Prince Peter Kropotkin and the American Henry David Thoreau. In the 1960s the "new left" produced another burst of anarchic sympathy that resulted in one especially trenchant defense of anarchism among many, Robert Paul Wolff's *In Defense of Anarchism.* There seems to be every evidence that in differing times and places the anarchist view will inevitably reemerge and pose its troubling accusation that all governments and nation states are as dispensable as they are immoral.[8] For example, there are environmental movements in contemporary Europe and the stubbornly resilient Solidarity movement in Poland, which display anarchic sympathies.

The cornerstone of the anarchist attack on the state and other centers of power is the assertion that each is deeply unethical in its very nature. Anarchists assert that all governments necessarily negate or at least limit individual rights and personhood, which are critical values. Governments are about laws, regulations, taxes, traffic lights, limitations on computer hackers, and much more, all of which are designed to restrict the individual, and they do so time and again all too effectively. Anarchists maintain that the only conclusion from this fact is that governments cannot be justified. They are tyrannical and corrosive of free and cooperative spirits.

Many people readily agree with the anarchists when they observe dictatorships or tyrannies in action. These governments surely block the individual at every turn. Many also agree when it comes to less authoritarian but still highly elitist or oligarchic states. Yet most of us want to make an exception of supposedly democratic regimes grounded in the free consent of individuals who constitute or sustain democracies. It is at this juncture that anarchists most strongly insist that all governments, including allegedly democratic ones, unacceptably curtail individual freedom. Wolff, Thoreau, and Kropotkin all maintain that majority rule means turning over to the majority or its agents in the political system the right and the power to decide what is best for each of us. Tyranny of the majority is still tyranny to its victims. It takes away from every individual the ultimate authority to rule over his or her own life. They insist that beneath the trappings of democracy lies the immoral, enduring reality that in theory and practice democracy involves the surrender of individual sovereignty.

If we share the anarchist's concern with individual liberty, as most of us do, it becomes obvious that the political theory of anarchism makes a powerful moral objection to states and governments. They are indeed restrictive and coercive, as are all institutions. There is an exaggeration here, however, that is important to explore. Anarchists tend to be monistic in their virtual obsession with personal freedom. There are other values worth pursuing. For example, we might want to have security for our person and property. Many people would say that this is as vital as individual freedom and argue that only (the right kind of) government can provide it effectively. All of us have to accept a balance among the many values we wish to maximize. Liberty is not the only objective for most persons and they willingly give up a good deal of it in order to gain security, among other things.

Even if we support the anarchists' sympathy for radical freedom above all else, it is still not clear that we should choose to have no state. Unless we are tremendously optimistic about human capacity for voluntary cooperation and for the avoidance of conflict, we may doubt that anarchy will be a condition that is nearly as fruitful for freedom as it might be for the tyranny of a few strong people over many weak ones. We suspect that the absence of government might bring as much chaos as consensus, particularly in an era when electronic eavesdropping and great capabilities for manipulating government and private files are available to any computer-literate person.

A second anarchist argument concentrates on the irrelevance of past history in estimating future possibilities for anarchic achievement. Anarchists declare that the fact that the state has been a central part of human experience in almost all known history does not prove that we could not do without it. Nor does it establish that governments are ethical. After all, murder is an inescapable part of the human story, but this fact neither proves that we must have murder in the future nor convinces us that murder is a good thing. Anarchists charge that statists suffer from twin errors. They lack sufficient confidence in human possibilities under better conditions in the time ahead, and they frequently, if erroneously, confuse what has existed with what is right.

Certainly the anarchists are correct in pointing out that there is no necessary connection between what is ethical and current practice. Unless, however, there is a great deal more research, yielding convincing evidence that it is coercive institutions that cause people to be uncooperative, the lack of past anarchic communities (except for small-scale experiments) should warn against a naive acceptance of these anarchist claims. They well may be right, but at the very least much more evidence needs to be accumulated before we are entitled to draw firm conclusions.

A further dimension to the anarchist case is that, despite what many believe, government is not a practical way to regulate human affairs, especially since there is a feasible alternative available. As anarchists read the record, the legacy of the state is an account of unrelieved human exploitation, robbery, murder, and denial of human liberty and creativity. They point to the world's slums, to the ever-spiraling crime rate, to wars, to concentration camps, and to prisons. Everywhere they look they see the denial of the human spirit accomplished under the false banner of government and its alleged benefits. They claim that people react to tyrannical, organized oppression by adapting to it, by being oppressive and violent.

The anarchist says that there is another, better way that is surprisingly practical. Most anarchists from Kropotkin to Wolff never shared Thoreau's concept of anarchism as a lonely, purely individualistic journey. They say that human beings, when freed from the stunting oppression of governments and police, will come together in cooperative communities, working and living in harmony as social individuals. When freed from hostile competition, people recognize their basic commonality, which leads to solidarity and cooperation. For them, free cooperation is the pragmatic answer to impractical government. It is what people will do if only allowed to do so.

This anarchist vision is attractive, but so is the stance of those who accept the necessity of government. Despite their protestations, anarchists are too confident about the possibility of finding an alternative to the state. To be sure, there are cooperative as well as competitive aspects of the human personality, but the vision of an automatically cooperative society, once coercive institutions are abolished, is as open to doubt as the faith of the conservatives that humans function best in a rigid hierarchy. Perhaps socialization has made us more competitive than we have to be, and this reflects on our governments. But government can be good or bad, coercive or liberating. It serves as an agency for conflict resolution in areas of public policy involving group competition, and it can allocate resources of public need as easily as it can bully, make war, and suppress minorities. Since the historical record of government is mixed, instead of condemning (or accepting) states as a whole, we feel it is more appropriate to realize that large-scale organizations, although inevitably valuable, are coercive and to ask whether that coercion can be minimized.

The more realistic anarchists insist that a combination of intense education and powerful social pressure can replace police and jails in most circumstances. They do not rely on a chimerical goodness of humanity. They argue that a society with a rigorous consensus needs nothing else to maintain its integrity and safety. They may be right, but the result is hardly coincident with the classic anarchist objective of expansive human choice. In a very real sense, these communities may not have an organized government, but they will be trading the prospects of a social tyranny for a political one. Neither is desirable, but political institutions are more visible and easier to control than social tyranny.

We must also note the growing complexity of human societies with vast populations, intricate economies, and increasing institutional differentiation to cope with them. Strong states and active governments can and do assist in directing and controlling this complexity. Government agencies like Conrail in the United States can bring economic order out of private chaos. It is questionable whether a decentralized anarchist order can manage economic life in the populous modern age without dismantling productive infrastructures at a high cost in standards of living. Nor is it entirely clear how an anarchist society could handle all the important welfare functions that modern governments assume. In a world of sharply reduced gross national product, where would the means be found to aid the old, the sick, and the handicapped? Moreover, recent experience in famine-ravaged lands of Africa and South Asia suggests that even human survival may be sacrificed when there is no efficient government to provide basic services (as basic as the construction and maintenance of transportation infrastructures to get foodstuffs from the docks to the starving people inland) in the absence or failure of private means.

We cannot easily get away from the state. It is a viable if not reliable means toward helpful, responsive social life. But there can be no better defense for the existence of a state than its record of practical accomplishments. As a means and not an absolute end in itself, the test of the state is what a government does for us. The immense value of the anarchist position is that it reminds us that government is no automatic or divine good. Nor is its record of performance, now and in the past, always a flattering or reassuring one. We frequently need organized government as a practical matter, but we also must heed the anarchist warning that it carries frequent dangers with it. As we turn toward democracy as the most sensible form of government in this regard, let us remember that it is precisely because democracy comes so close to satisfying the principal anarchist questions about the state, while simultaneously providing many of the benefits of the state, that we are democrats. Thus, we owe the anarchists a debt of gratitude.

DEMOCRATIC LEGITIMACY AND ITS CRITICS

The analysis above leads us deeper into the questions of legitimate government. Our answers suggest other questions, which set the stage for our analysis of democracy in both its philosophical and institutional dimensions. Once the moral rationale for democracy has been established, our attention can turn to the subject of our next chapter, giving those moral principles life through appropriate democratic institutions.

The key moral questions in government concern legitimacy, the characteristic of being just and authoritative. Democratic government is no exception. Either it is based on a legitimate concept of authority or it should not exist. Ultimately, legitimacy asks two disarmingly simple questions that have radical implications: Who should rule? Who has the moral right to rule and why?

History contains an unending record of human struggle over these fundamental questions of politics and political theory. Once government exists and has been justified in our minds, this problem is inevitable. Consider all the wars that have been fought over this issue, the revolutions undertaken, the lives "given," as humans contested the right to govern. From the beginning of written records to the latest African coup, the struggle to establish authoritative leadership is a perennial one.

This section investigates the problem of legitimate authority, exploring several of the many viewpoints that thinkers over time have had about who should rule, ultimately endorsing the principles that are the foundations of democratic theory. All perspectives on legitimate authority contain two inseparable parts. One describes who should rule, while the other names the qualification or criterion by which the ruler's legitimate authority is maintained. The crucial matter is the second part. One qualification or another can justify several, if not all, answers to the query of who should govern. For example, if the appropriate standard for legitimate authority is popular consent, then one could support a host of very different systems under that banner, anything from participatory government to the quite elitist rule of an elected few. It could include the New England town meeting, participatory democracy in a Swiss canton, Britain's elitist prime ministerial rule, or Lenin's democratic centralism. If a rigorous standard of consent that demands considerable, long-term, direct manifestation of support is used, perhaps no government in the world today would pass muster.

The vital issue for political theory, then, is not so much who rules as by what authority may anyone rule, the problem of legitimacy. What conditions give governors, whoever they are and whatever form of government they constitute, an ethical right to exercise power? By what values do particular polities, especially democracies, claim moral validity?

Democratic Legitimacy

The most popular, if not the sole standard of legitimate authority is the democratic one. It holds that governments are legitimate only when they receive and retain the free consent of the governed. Just how much consent, through what forms of participation, is necessary is the question. There is a feeling that provisions for passive popular participation, complete with coerced shows of enthusiasm at mass rallies, or voting rights in choiceless elections are not enough, partly because they do not open sufficient alternatives to the populace. In the United States, for example, there are elections with at least some range of choice, but some critics wonder whether consent exists through regularized elections, when over 50 percent of the adult population does not bother to vote for president and over three quarters of them stay home for critical primary elections. On the other hand, the Tanzanians and the Soviets, among others, claim that a one-party election can be sufficiently democratic, while the Swiss hold referenda on a broad range of complex policy questions several times a year. These points of disagreement among democrats lead to questions. How often should elections be held? How much choice is adequate? Must there be plenty of opportunities to leave the country? (Consent is discussed further in Chapter 7, on political obligation.)

Democrats do not agree, either, on what the support of a democratic criterion of authority may rest. Some argue that because we are all moral equals as persons, we should play an equal role in approving who rules us. Others talk in terms of natural rights, maintaining that we all have the right by nature to approve who shall govern us. Still others declare that all people are more or less wise, certainly wise enough to choose who should exercise power over them, and a society is wrong as well as foolish to ignore what we may call this right of common wisdom. All of these justifications stipulate that the foundation of legitimacy must be the honor and respect that we owe every person. This concept continues to animate and engage people in their political deliberations, as we saw in 1982 when the Canadians united on a new democratic constitution based on this, in spite of strong suspicions engendered by French versus English animosities.

Even though democrats disagree on many procedural points, they are united in a strong consensus about the substance of democracy. One of the most fundamental points of agreement is the belief that the same equality that justifies a political system based on the consent of the governed supports scrupulously maintained rights of its citizens. All parties must have real access to a stall in the free marketplace of ideas, all opinions must be considered, aspiring alternative rulers and their party organizations must be able to operate freely, and elections must be open to genuine contest. The people must be able to go to the ballot box and change an entire government, if they choose to do so, on the basis of accurate and complete knowledge of policies and personalities and electoral rules of the game that allow truly general and free elections. Governors elected with little or no opposition (or elected to parts of a system that largely remains unchanged after the election) cannot be said to have gained authentic consent of the governed. Perhaps they would have been defeated if an opponent had existed or was in a fair contest with proportionately equal electoral resources. Democracy requires that the determination be made at the ballot box, not in supposition and after-the-fact charges and countercharges.

There are some other fundamental principles that all democrats unite on, as well. Even though democrats demonstrate remarkable diversity on what institutional forms to embrace to enfranchise people, they share the conviction that people should have the right to select their rulers. They do so because they believe that governments are only instruments to satisfy those ends. To democrats, governments ought to exist as tools through which people can establish and nourish moral relationships to each other in the political sphere. Governments have no absolute justifications of their own, and thus the individual is worth more than the state. The policy implications of this liberal democratic value are enormous, as we shall see in the chapter on liberty, which follows our analysis of democracy. The Western notion that no person, leader or commoner, is above the law flows directly from this basic democratic principle.

Democrats also feel that people are fully capable of reasoning on at least the broad policy outlines of what modern democratic polities face, even in today's frighteningly complex world. They maintain that if people are given the education, the information, and the liberty to act on their capabilities, they can do at least as well in policy making as elites do especially when they do not have the educational tools to understand complex problems, when they are lied to by administrators, or when the pressure of events or tyranny prevents thorough deliberations. It is no surprise that this applies to masses in the policy-making process, as well. Genuine democrats believe that all people can do a superior job if they have the tools and the opportunity to use them. Modern communications technology (especially television, the telephone, and the computer) can solve the physical problem of getting information out and back from citizens, making the democratic polities of the twenty-first century as potentially cozy and manageable as the tiny democratic city-state of Athens in the fifth century B.C.

Of course, an aware citizenry requires good political education and reasonably objective and thorough mass media. Much more needs to be accomplished in these areas all over the world. If people can learn the intricacies of a zone pass defense in professional football, they can learn the intricacies of a missile defense as well. Whether a large group or a small group of people makes decisions in a polity, decisions must be made, and it is people who must make them. Democrats suggest that not only should decision makers be well equipped to make those decisions, irrespective of the size of the group, but that it makes moral sense that those who are affected and pay for polities should be given the opportunity to have an informed say in their policy processes, whether directly or indirectly. Empirically, there is no evidence that informed masses make more mistakes than equally informed elites.

Some democrats go further and insist that people ought to have maximum feasible participation in self-rule. Since they can rule themselves, they should do so. People are worthy and can be trained to become sophisticated legislators, especially if they are given the potent incentive of power over their own destinies to induce them to be good legislators. Therefore, there are neither insurmountable normative nor empirical impediments to the process of self-rule. The principle is radically simple: Because each worthy person has a functionally equivalent stake in, benefits from, and contributes to democratic societies, each person should have a functionally equivalent say in either the actual policy decisions (for direct democrats) or in who should make them (for indirect democrats.)

Finally, it is worthwhile to note again that in spite of broad agreement on what constitutes democracy, democrats have substantial disagreements about the details of implementing them, the subject of the following chapter. This is not a problem unique to democracy, however. Critics of the democratic form of legitimacy (proponents of competing principles of legitimacy) are more united in their opposition to democracy than in anything else. Their disputes about how to implement their principles are generally deeper than those of the democrats.

Alternatives to the Democratic Form of Legitimacy

There is no shortage of criticisms of democracy and its principles of legitimacy, but all share even more flaws than do democratic concepts. We recognize that democracy is far from perfect, but we cannot help but nod assent to the comment widely attributed to the British Conservative leader Winston Churchill: "Democracy is the worst form of government known to man, except for all the others."

An alternative concept of legitimate authority argues that tradition provides proper authority. This perspective is dominant in past and present tribal societies, where rulership is grounded in practices that are taken for granted and seem to have originated in the indefinable past. It also surfaces in combination with other ideas in justifications of Arab monarchies and the Israeli right to settle occupied lands in the Middle East today. In fact, almost all stable societies depend on this version of legitimacy to some degree, though few "modern" societies make it the lynchpin of just authority, as monarchies and some tribal governments do.

Certainly in the United States or England, the ways in which the rulers are inaugurated are highly traditional. Even the ceremonies surrounding the ratification of the 1982 democratic constitution of Canada were presided over by the queen, as well as the prime minister. The historical familiarity attached to the four-year process of a presidential term helps us feel that the present is linked to the past—and all is well. The rich tradition that surrounds—the drafting of the Declaration of Independence and the Constitution by the Founding Fathers, the defense of the Union by Lincoln, and so on—all constitute a tapestry of history that is the backdrop of our present-day government and partially sustains it. Politicians constantly try to clothe themselves in it in attempts to endow themselves and their policies with traditional legitimacy, no matter how far-fetched that may seem. And it often works. The bitterness and divisiveness that characterized the home front during and for a decade after the Vietnam War are being smoothed over in a process of historical revisionism in the mid-1980s that placed a Vietnam-era soldier in the Tomb of the Unknown Soldier. It also saw President Reagan use Memorial Day holidays to justify his aggressive stance toward the Soviet Union in the "patriotic successes" of our Vietnam intervention, thereby attempting to associate himself with the noble warriors and causes of U.S. history.

There is nothing uniquely American about this process, of course. The greater the role that tradition plays in defining the just authority of a political order, the more likely that system will be to resist changes. Indeed, to the traditionalists change is a great enemy, for each change brings a break with the sacrosanct past. Edmund Burke, the great eighteenth-century traditionalist, argued that we ought to preserve the main outlines of our political past because they have been proven by the past. If we did not let tradition govern us, we would have a dictator or a majoritarian mob, both of them frightening tyrants. The people cannot be trusted, because they do not have historically developed wisdom, and dictators cannot be trusted because they rule for themselves, not for the good of the nation. Neither of these options could possibly match the practical wisdom embodied in human tradition over the centuries that created our current political forms and ideas. Nor did Burke think that the massive changes sought by radicals in the French Revolution would endure in a regime likely to be a stable form of order. Old habits would not be swiftly displaced by the new-fangled or leveling ideas of reformers. Modern traditionalists agree.[9]

In the traditionalist outlook, then, there is a deep sense that the past is wiser than the fleeting notions of the present, whether interpreted by rulers or by majorities. While the implication here is that the traditionalists are both conservative and automatically antidemocratic, this is not always true. Traditionalists may grudgingly support any form of stable government, from rule by tribal chieftain to governance by the British Parliament, as long as each state respects its own national traditions, even in the face of needed policy or institutional changes in the present that are incongruent with them. They will support these kinds of governments as long as they do not give the power to rule over to "mobs in the street," regardless of their demands.

Tradition does have its stabilizing, practical purposes for almost all societies, but as a moral form of authority it is flawed. Traditionalism flounders when it tries to support its guiding proposition, that what has been done or justified in the past is moral for today. One may make a utilitarian case for this supposition, as Burke did by stressing its stabilizing benefits, but then every aspect of a tradition must be carefully scrutinized to make sure each has positive pragmatic effects. This is a serious and worthy argument, but when tradition is simply accepted as a matter of faith, then it is without foundation as a basis for legitimacy. It does not follow that just because something has been done in the past, it is right to do now. The past is not a moral position. It is a dim fact, but is in no way ethical itself.

If a traditionalist theory of legitimate authority fails, another theory raises different objections to democracy. Divine or natural-law tests of proper authority hold that any regime rules in a legitimate manner only if there is evidence that God (or the gods) or nature "licenses" it. Advocates praise these standards, because they are transcendental norms whose moral sovereignty can scarcely be impugned, since they are self-evident. Old Testament Israel justified its monarchy under a vision that God's reluctant endorsement of monarchy and His provision of a set of laws made the regime acceptable. Even into the last century many monarchs justified their rule by claiming they had divine right to govern, that God had selected them to exercise authority and denied anyone a right to interfere. Thomas Jefferson, in the Declaration of Independence, assumed that nature and God were the ultimate standards that applied in any decision about whether or not a government was legitimate. This was, in fact, a standard view of many of the thinkers of that era on both sides of the Atlantic. Thoreau, too, looked to nature, to the whistling of the wind in the trees and the free rush of a brook in springtime, when he concluded that nature decreed that all governments as he knew them were illegitimate.[10]

These criteria of legitimacy are not heard so often in this era or in secular states with no official faith in God or nature. We should remember, however, that many continue to look to God for guidance in politics, as in other aspects of life, in spite of the biblical admonition that God helps those who help themselves. The resurgent Christian Right in the United States is a good example. Some modern-day ecology movements appear to be the new prophets of nature, judging governmental legitimacy by their policy devotion to preserving nature, as the Green Party in the Federal Republic of Germany does. It is quite impossible to prove that these tests are invalid. Yet, unless we know personally, as a matter of faith, that a particular god or image of nature is the correct one, it is impossible to respect any general reliance on this standard. In the world today it is hard to find much unity on a single transcendental or natural standard of legitimacy and equally hard to get many people even to concede that there might be such a standard. One or another such standard might be our personal norm of proper political authority, but few societies, including those in the Third World, can or will use this criterion today. Regimes like Iran under Khomeini are a prominent exception.

We may well regret this fact, and perhaps we should, for without ultimate standards in politics we may seem adrift. We should not, however, underestimate the human capacity to formulate tentative answers, provisional reasons, existential choices, or practical resolutions as guides in political theory and political life. The only answers are not ultimate answers or utter relativism.

A final alternative conception of proper authority in perennial conflict with democracy focuses on the right of those who have special knowledge or qualifications to rule. Its proponents claim that only experts should direct human society. They maintain that only demonstration of the appropriate knowledge should earn one legitimacy as a governor. Plato, for instance, contended that Athens would be far better and more legitimately governed if it were controlled by those few who knew what Plato declared to be the truth. It was morally wrong as far as he was concerned to let the masses rule, because they did not know the good from the evil or the merely tempting. In our age, B. F. Skinner supports a similar ideal—rule by experts—as his utopia, *Walden Two*, shows so clearly.[11]

Variations between these two examples, however, reveal the crucial complication attendant to this theory of legitimacy. Those who cling to the standard that only the knowledgeable should govern constantly disagree over what knowledge sanctifies legitimacy. Skinner's behavioral managers have a certain form of psychological knowledge and skill that he contends is the proper bulwark for their authority to lead their community. The knowledge that Plato considers essential for his philosopher-kings is quite another type of knowledge, knowledge of the transcendant forms of truth and morality, the ultimate and objective rules of the universe. In the face of disputations over who is truly wise and what is truly wisdom, we must hesitate before following any of the claimants of special governing knowledge, whether they are astrologers, natural scientists, social scientists, or clergymen. We may doubt their legitimacy, because we have no reason to accept one or another of their assertions of expertise in matters governmental simply because they are experts in certain fields.

Aristotle, a student of Plato, developed this theme. He challenged anyone to demonstrate to him that in matters of basic public policy any citizen, however wise in whatever ways, knew more than anyone else what is best for him. His homely analogy that only someone who wears a shoe knows whether or not it pinches is still a powerful, indeed decisive, argument against the view that expertise should confer governing legitimacy. Aristotle did not mean that there should not be temporary governors or public officials, nor do we suggest that some technical matters may not be best directed by experts from many fields, under the supervision of popular authority. Instead, his point and our point is that it is simply impossible to prove that anybody knows what is best for us better than we do.[12] We are all experts about ourselves and each of us has the same stake in our political community. Thus, each of us has an equal claim to participate in political power. Government, after all, covers a comprehensive range of issues. Its policy needs are far greater than any single type of expertise and respond best to deliberation among many viewpoints. What is required is simply a commitment to disagree in an agreeable manner and according to a commonly accepted set of rules.

There are other versions of just political authority, but these four—democracy, tradition, transcendent norms, and expertise—are the most serious. Our view is that the democratic one is the most convincing. It is a doctrine that holds that respect for every person requires a form of political authority that is based on consent. No state is legitimate that does not use the participation and opinion of its citizens and thus exists for the needs of its citizens and not vice versa. This concept of legitimate authority forms the basis for a form of government that allows for the mutual satisfaction of reasonable public needs and opportunities, while it minimizes the coercion inherent in states that the anarchists legitimately oppose. In the final analysis, the more we become the state, the less likely we are to coerce ourselves.

This appealing democratic view is widely shared in the world today, though it is by no means universal. Thus, a UNESCO study not too long ago showed that almost all states asserted that they are democratic, as democracy is understood by them. Even if we insist that there can be no genuine democracy without implementation of the common principles of democracy we have mentioned earlier, many nations would still pass the test, though the majority would not. Democracy appears to be alive, if not well. Our attention now turns to how to make it well.

NOTES

1. "Epicurus" in *The Stoic and Epicurean Philosophers*, ed. W. J. Oates (New York: Modern Library, 1940).

2. Reinhold Niebuhr, *The Children of Light and the Children of Darkness* (New York: Scribners, 1944).

3. Harold Lasswell, *The Political Writings* (New York: Free Press, 1951).

4, Hannah Arendt, *On Revolution* (New York: Viking, 1963); Albert Camus, *The Rebel* (New York: Vintage, 1956).

5. Bernard Berelson et al., *Voting* (Chicago: University of Chicago Press, 1954), pp. 311-23.

6. B. F. Skinner, *Walden Two* (New York: Macmillan, 1948); Lao-Tzu, *The Book of Tao* (New York: Peter Pauper Press, 1962); Leo Tolstoy, *The Kingdom of God is Within You* (New York: Noonday Press, 1961).

7. Henry David Thoreau, *Walden and Other Writings* (New York: Random House, 1950).

8. Peter Kropotkin, *Mutual Aid* (New York: McClure, 1907); Thoreau, "Civil Disobedience," in *Walden*; Robert Paul Wolff, *In Defense of Anarchy* (New York: Harper & Row, 1970).

9. Edmund Burke, *Reflections on the Revolution in France* (Indianapolis: Library of Liberal Arts, 1955).

10. Old Testament, *Kings* and *Chronicles*; The Declaration of Independence; Thoreau, *Walden*.

11. Plato, *The Collected Dialogues*, ed. E. Hamilton and H. Cairns (Princeton, N.J.: Princeton University Press, 1961); Skinner, *Walden Two*.

12. Aristotle, *The Politics* (New York: Oxford University Press, 1962).

SUGGESTIONS FOR SUPPLEMENTARY READING

Politics

Crawford, Alan. *Thunder on the Right*. New York: Pantheon, 1980.

Crick, Bernard. *In Defense of Politics*. Chicago: University of Chicago Press, 1962.

Hill, David B., and Norman R. Luttberg. *Trends in American Electoral Behavior*, 2nd ed. Itasca, Ill.: Peacock, 1983.

Thoreau, Henry D. *Walden and Other Writings*. New York: Random House, 1950.

Organization and Anarchy

Camus, Albert. *The Rebel* New York: Vintage Press, 1956.

Thoreau, Henry D. *Civil Disobedience*. Many publications.

Wolff, Robert Paul. *In Defense of Anarchy*. New York: Harper & Row, 1970.

Democratic Legitimacy

Aristotle. *The Politics*. Many publications.

Bone, Hugh and Austin Ranny. *Politics and Voters*, 5th ed. New York: McGraw-Hill, 1981.

Burke, Edmund. *Reflections on the Revolution in France*. New York: Library of Liberal Arts, 1955.

Hill, David B., and Norman R. Luttberg. *Trends in American Electoral Behavior*, 2nd ed. Itasca, Ill.: Peacock, 1983.

Jefferson, Thomas. *Notes on the State of Virginia*. Many publications.

Pateman, Carole. *Participation and Democratic Theory*. Cambridge: Cambridge University Press, 1970.

Pitkin, Hanna Fenichel. *The Concept of Representation*. Berkeley: University of California Press, 1972.

Plamenatz, John. *Democracy and Illusion*. London: Longman, 1977.

Plato. *The Republic*. Many publications.

Rejai, M. *Democracy*. New York: Atherton, 1967.

Spitz, David. *Patterns of Anti-Democratic Thought*, rev. ed. New York: Free Press, 1965.

Spitz, Elaine. *Majority Rule*. Chatham, New Jersey: Chatham House, 1984.

Taylor, Richard W., Ed. *Linking The Governors and the Governed*. Kent, Ohio: Kent Popular Press, 1981.

3

Concepts of Democracy

Even if it is possible to construct a convincing case for democracy as the most attractive kind of government, how can we decide which of the many competing types of democracy is the ideal one? Democracy means somewhat contrasting things in various nations and cultures. It undeniably takes multiple institutional shapes. As we have seen, even if we eliminate regimes that do not approximate anything we might call democratic, since they lack competitive elections, political liberties, checks on abusive power, and in some cases, anything recognizably democratic except the slightest pretense of honoring the norm of consent of the governed, there are still many that have some claim to the label "democracy."

Political theorists identify at least four main versions of democracy today: pluralism, participatory democracy, populism, and democratic socialism. We shall explore each in turn.

PLURALISM

Perhaps the most widespread concept of democracy in the West today is what we may call pluralism. Most Western nations in practice, including the United States, are fairly close to the pluralist model. Pluralism is the idea that democracy concerns leadership of citizens and groups within a constitutional framework. Its proponents insist that democracy requires universal suffrage, selection of rulers or representatives by the voters from among two or more competing elites or parties, provision for extensive political liberties and organized interest groups, and regularized checks on leaders. It emphasizes leadership, while holding that opportunity for political participation (to the degree a citizen chooses) must be broad. It specifically leaves policy making to the ruling elites, while reserving to the public the right to select among the contending elites and to join pressure groups to promote their policy views. Two aspects of pluralism are especially important—leadership and interest-group representation. Each has its particular advocates—and critics.

Leadership

Leadership enthusiasts praise it as eminently practical. Furthermore, they insist that it reflects a mature reaction to the lessons about human behavior taught by modern social science and modern history. They argue also that this aspect of pluralism promotes long-term stability better than any of the alternatives. These propositions are important and we need to examine them in detail.

Its defenders maintain that pluralism's emphasis on leadership shows its practicality by its provision for a division of labor that is absolutely mandatory in large, modern industrial and technological societies. Life has grown so complex and societies so large that it is impossible for each citizen to be involved in major policy decisions. Leaders are essential. Moreover, too much popular involvement in policy matters would obviously be unwise, since expert knowledge is needed in considering so many policies, from weapons systems to pollution management—expertise that only leaders can possess or mobilize.

Overall, the conclusion many democratic theorists reach in our age is that leadership is vital and that pluralism best acknowledges this inexorable reality. Some thinkers, such as Robert Heilbroner in *The Human Prospect*, underline this concern in the light of what they feel is the uniquely dangerous situation of modern times. They note that humankind today, as never before, faces the issue of survival. Nuclear annihilation is a distinct possibility. Population growth in some parts of the world threatens to overwhelm the planet's distribution systems and perhaps its productive capacities, as well. Ecological dangers are present everywhere, and disastrous ecological destruction threatens many peoples. In such a situation, these theorists think vigorous political leadership will be necessary. Some are by no means convinced that any democracy can provide enough leadership to tackle these challenges. They are certain, however, that only a form of democracy that provides strong leadership has even a chance to meet them.

Others note another, related feature of pluralism that they believe makes it the best democracy we can get. For them pluralism is attractive because its provision for leadership is so congruent with what we know about human behavior in politics. They take note of the avalanche of findings in modern social science research which demonstrate that the average American citizen (and citizens in other democracies too) has only a minimal interest in the political process, has surprisingly little information about it, and is prepared to devote scant time to becoming politically informed. Many thinkers believe that a more participatory system would demand too much time from disinterested and often uninformed average citizens. It would "take too many nights" and interfere with bowling, family, television, or other activities.

For pluralists their version of democracy is the way out of this problem. It nicely balances an often disinterested and ignorant citizenry with a form of government in which not a great deal is asked of most people other than an occasional vote. The whole is a system that provides the opportunity to govern for an informed minority who care deeply about politics, while preserving for the large majority the chance to select their leaders, undisturbed by any substantial demands on their time or energy.

Some proponents of pluralism go on to applaud its leadership side by publicly worrying about the danger of mass political involvement (often at the behest of unscrupulous nonpluralist rulers). Some recall the success Hitler, Mussolini, and Stalin had in creating frenzied and dangerous mass responses in politics. Others cite current examples of mass movements, such as the Khomeini crusade in Iran. Still others draw from the world of myth and symbolism in politics to reinforce their unease about irrational mass behavior in politics. Pluralists observe that their democracy does not welcome the politics of mass action and mass movements and thus avoids outbreaks of mass human irrationalism, often caused by elite manipulation. Pluralism depends, instead, on responsible leaders, elected by voters who expect leaders to govern subject to constitutional checks.

Finally, pluralists contend that their theory's stress on leadership is good because leadership ordinarily helps achieve a societal balance between stability and the openness to change that every society needs. It is no surprise that pluralists often worry about preserving stability, nor that in their view leaving much of actual governing in the hands of leaders will maximize stability (and promote "responsible" change). Indeed, pluralists are frequently identified with the outlines (if not all the practices or details) of such modern neopluralist societies as Great Britain, the United States, and Australia and they want to preserve them. Moreover, they are sure that nations that shift from a leadership-oriented democracy to a much more participatory system would be so subject to oscillating (and possibly irrational) popular moods that effective, stable management of the vexing political challenges of our day would disappear. Its replacement would be a dangerous politics of instability.

It should be noted, however, that pluralists also believe that leadership is the ideal means to foster changes. They realize full well that political systems that do not change at all become brittle and incompetent to master the conflicts and tensions of our time. Thus pluralists often favor changes—in elites and in policies. They do so, however, with an appreciation for informed, rational leadership and gradual, incremental adjustments, which they believe pluralism encourages—and which they insist also promote stability.

Group Representation

Our Founding Fathers looked askance at pressure groups and even at political parties, which they called "factions." Adams, Hamilton, Madison, and most of the rest bewailed the inclination of people to ally in political groups, because this encouraged selfishness in politics. They felt the focus should be on the common interest and the common good. Many leaders did realize that the tendency toward interest groups in politics was inevitable, if regrettable. A thinker such as Thomas Jefferson, who accepted organized parties and even interest groups as natural and often healthy, was exceptional. Over time, however, attitudes changed, and after World War II interest-group pluralism received thorough investigation, most notably through David Truman's classic, *The Governmental Process,* and there have been many ardent celebrations of its contribution to any vibrant democracy.

Pluralists who accent this side of pluralist democracy often cite three positive impacts of pressure groups. First, they argue, pluralist groups create substantial representation that is as meaningful as one can expect in the modern world. These interest groups allow organized citizens an input into the political decision-making process greater than can be gained from the electoral process alone. They permit groups of citizens to have a say in the ongoing day-to-day legislative and administrative decisions that are the stuff of ordinary politics. At the same time, the group process takes account of people's limited interest in and time for politics, government complexities, and mass movements.

Most members of groups need to do little. It is the leaders of the interest groups, their staffs, and their lobbyists who do the actual work of representation for their memberships. In this feature of pluralism, too, a few with time and professional expertise serve the many.

To all this enthusiasm for the increase in democracy that they believe interest groups afford, pluralists add a second aspect they find attractive: the practicality that organized interests make possible. We know that pluralists pride themselves on being practical and scorn forms of democracy they judge to be impossible to achieve. They insist that everyone must understand that few citizens can exercise much influence *as individuals.* Nations are too large and people too busy for that.

Individuals must and in pluralism can and do adjust to this reality. They form groups—which pluralist democracy encourages. Moreover, these groups provide a realistic check on the other fact of life that reigns in any government, democratic or not: the reality of elites. Once again, single individuals cannot ordinarily check irresponsible leaders. Only organized and powerful groups can do that, and in pluralism they are, in fact, the main practical limiting influence on rulers.

Finally, pluralists return to the theme of the optimum balance of stability and change. Groups ordinarily operate, they contend, in a fashion that requires compromise among different interests and goals. This process of continual compromise produces change, but in a context of ongoing order that they welcome. For them compromise is attractive. They react angrily to those who scorn their politics of compromise as the sacrifice of principles. Compromise, pluralists believe, can produce not only a progressive stability but democratic representation in which almost all citizens get at least part of what they seek from the political system. To pluralists this is democracy at work.

PARTICIPATORY DEMOCRACY

Pluralism is, however, far from the only claimant to democracy. One alternative is participatory democracy: the idea that democracy is best only when it is exercised by people as directly as possible on the local or national level. The language of democratic politics records this perennial ideal of democracy: self-government, direct rule, community control, decentralization, neighborhood government, community standards. In the 1960s interest in participatory democracy underwent a revival that is as famous as it was controversial. Black power cries for community control, the birth of community action agencies, agitation for local police review boards and decentralized school systems, demand for "power to the people," student uprisings in places as different as Berkeley and Paris, even George Wallace's advocacy of decision by "plain [white] folks" all reminded Americans of the continued appeal of the ideal of direct democracy and decentralized politics. While this clamor has quieted down in the 1980s, interest remains and receives expression in the widespread support for neighborhood organizations, urban and rural cooperatives, and even condominium housing.

Enthusiasts of direct democracy consider it both morally persuasive and practical. They insist that democracy really lives only when citizens decide in assemblies or meetings, as directly as possible, what policies they want in their political system. They oppose turning over such decisions to those they see as remote elites, elected representatives and leaders of interest groups. For them democracy is dead whenever we surrender our self-government to pluralist elites of any form. While many primary democrats grant a need for central governments, national elections, and pressure groups, they seek to minimize them by decentralizing power and authority as much as possible by putting power into the hands of citizens themselves. Only when, they repeat, citizens are in actual control over their lives can democracy be said to exist.

Arguments for the moral validity of participatory democracy go back at least to Greece in the sixth century B.C. It is an idea far older than pluralism, and its critics, as Plato's bitter denunciation of the ideal shows, have lasted just as long. While democracy in any form hardly warmed the hearts of many of the great political philosophers of the past, some thinkers have been attracted to it, including Rousseau, Jefferson, John Stuart Mill, and John Dewey. None of them expected that we could have the ideal of participatory democracy fully realized. All pointed to factors such as numbers, territory, and human social characteristics that made complete participatory government, Rousseau's "government of the gods," unlikely. Still, these theorists considered expanded citizen involvement to be synonymous with good government and eminently practical as well. In the end they shared Pericles' and the Athenian democrats' faith that living democracy is participatory democracy.

Since primary democrats pose the most serious contemporary challenge to the established pluralist definition of democracy, consideration of participatory politics requires considerable discussion in order to indicate what many of the main points of dispute have been among the contending visions of democracy in our age. The participatory school begins, like its competitors, by claiming to exemplify the highest possible standard of representation. Primary democrats claim that the fullest and most immediate type of democracy is small-scale and personal in nature—in a word, direct. They feel that representation is a hollow substitute for personal, meaningful participaton in governmental affairs. Only direct self-government can make political institutions responsive in performance as well as name. They ridicule the pluralist position, maintaining that it is merely the principle of elective aristocracy. They claim that, once elected, an elite is free to dictate its will until it has to be on its best behavior in order to win the next election. They dismiss pluralist protestations about group representation, noting that few groups speak for their mass members as often as they do for their well-insulated elites. Participatory democrats also point out how many people (especially the poor and disadvantaged) have no group to pressure and lobby for their interests.

Pluralist thinkers, however, dispute the idea that community control is uniquely democratic or representative. They cite the lack of democracy in many small towns dominated by well-established elites, and they report the findings of small-groups studies that do not sustain the participatory democrats' vision of an equalitarian and free democracy. They continually return to their belief that leadership is a permanent feature in human affairs.

Moreover, pluralists remain convinced that direct self-government concentrates too exclusively on the goal of heightened participation. They contend that there are other values important for a successful democracy. For example, they admire efficiency and they see participatory democracy as a hopelessly inefficient instrument for a successful, functioning government.

This objection is obviously serious, but it bothers many direct democrats less than it does their critics. After all, many advocates of primary politics expect to continue to have a central government in their system. They note that small nations can have a central government with a large participatory element, as Switzerland does, and some have high hopes for the possible assistance that modern technology can render in this cause. More often, they stress that their central government could be and should be much smaller and much more responsive than it is now in almost all societies, democratic or not. At the same time, though, many participatory democrats profess that they are willing to sacrifice some efficiency for increased participation. Some go further and admit that their participatory democracy might be quite inefficient at least in the short run—but that is a risk they are willing to take as the trade-off for more democratic institutions.

There is also the pluralist suspicion that localism may frustrate a broader national will and thus turn out, ironically, to be quite undemocratic from a national perspective. National majorities may be overruled by local majorities that may not always be particularly kind or fair in their treatment of their own local minority. Pluralists question, for example, whether a powerful participatory system in the deep South might not allow bigots to flaunt U.S. civil rights laws with impunity, creating a form of tyranny over local blacks, or whether the factional hatreds associated with the Palestinian civil war might not be exacerbated by local control. Perhaps, indeed, institution of participatory politics would mean that public policy would be governed too much by selfish or fanatical local majorities.

Participatory democrats claim, with good reason, that the size of a government is not a guarantor of tyranny or of its absence. They believe a smaller, more responsive participatory democracy may be no worse than any other in regard to majority tyranny, while obviously better at the translation of reasoned public opinion into policy. Certainly, no form of democracy can easily solve clashes between majorities and minorities, a problem that will be dealt with more fully in Chapters 4 and 5 on liberty and equality.

Participatory democrats, then, feel that the potential benefits outweigh the possible risks of attempting primary government, or at least a drastic return of power from central to community governments. They appreciate that most societies all over the world appear to be moving toward greater centralization and they know that movement in the opposite direction would represent a gamble. They feel, however, that we must take risks if we are serious about democracy.

The debate over the policy advantages of a more participatory politics via local control has so far not been empirically resolved. One political scientist, Peter Eisinger, has surveyed the evidence available and concludes that there is a good deal of reason to be skeptical of uncritical assumptions about policy maximization through control sharing and primary politics. But the evidence is still meager, and many participatory democrats insist that policy questions are not the primary issue. They maintain that what really counts is human dignity, which they contend is best served in radically responsive polities. Most enthusiasts of participatory politics offer this justification for their political theory, pointedly accenting the psychological advantages of primary politics. The essence of the argument is that only participatory democracy can develop the human personality; that other forms of democracy are merely mechanisms of governance instead of vehicles for human growth.

This has long been a theme of participatory democrats. Many traditional theorists, starting with Pericles in ancient Athens, have claimed that political participation improves—even ennobles—humankind. John Stuart Mill, Ernest Barker, John Dewey, and David Lilienthal have been among the most exuberant celebrants of participatory democracy's potential for human growth in the past 150 years, but there have been many others. Like their present-day successors, however, they are vague about how the "development of human personality" is to take place except by the natural process of human interaction. The results of the process, however, receive a multitude of descriptions. Participatory government will bring to every person "a spiritual yield . . . a renewed sense that the individual counts." Each will attain the chance to be truly "human" or realize the "human way of life." People will gain an expanded moral sensitivity, greater "independence of mind" and increased social talents. In this process primary democracy becomes, in Dewey's words, a "way of life." The total process may be complex, but the result will be a new life, a new reality for people, on a plane of achievement and satisfaction never known before.

Most of the literature produced by contemporary social scientists attracted to participatory democracy is in a direct line of descent from these older arguments. Like previous views, it praises the ideal for its potential, which Peter Bachrach describes as "the full development of individual capacities." The literature repeatedly contends that active participation in an environment that encourages an involved citizen will guarantee a better person.

Defenders of the hypothesis that the growth of a "better" person is the great attraction of participatory democracy take one of two approaches. There are those who announce the truth of this empirical claim rather than endeavor to substantiate it. They make numerous but vague references to participatory politics as the means to unfold the "intellectual, emotional and moral capacities" of people, or as the guarantee of advances in human "dignity." These objectives are impressive, but there is often scant exploration or explication of what they mean or what their relation is to known empirical data. Some advocates of participatory democracy are considerably more scholarly, however, and deserve to be taken quite seriously. They devote ample attention to the empirical basis for their psychological case. For example, Carole Pateman's *Participation and Democratic Theory* notes a considerable literature that suggests that a sense of personal efficacy, or self-esteem, does tend to develop with involvement in significant areas of life. Other studies reveal that those who take part in specific participatory political situations may attain a greater sense of ego strength, even when their participatory institution falls far short of the primary democratic model. For instance, D. R. Marshall's study of a community action board in Los Angeles claims that even though the experimental effort in participation collapsed in unequivocal failure, the poor who did become entwined in the board's mesh of activity became more self-assured personalities.

Another side to the argument for the "human" advantages of participatory politics concentrates on the human values supposedly promoted by (as well as manifested in) a participatory society. Two norms in particular are often cited by proponents. They say that participatory politics promotes both authentic individualism and considerable community. This is important because most primary democrats believe that community and individualism are both inextricably linked with the good life: Each is valuable as part of what makes a life worth living and each is intimately connected with the other. They believe that without community there can be no genuine individualism and vice versa.

On the one hand, the pronounced anarchistic tones of many primary democrats are unmistakable. They often talk of individual liberation and stress the absolute importance of individual moral autonomy. At the same time they are convinced that such autonomy can be achieved only in cooperation with others in community, including participatory politics.

All of this sounds very insubstantial to social scientists who are not sympathetic to participatory democracy. It often seems to them to be a mass of assertions about what would be nice. To them, primary democracy for a nation-state remains hopelessly impractical, whatever the personal or ideological ends it undertakes to realize and in spite of breakthroughs in communications technology. Some critics acknowledge that participatory politics is abstractly the best form of democracy, while others deny this claim, but they agree that participatory democracy in modern societies is an impossible ideal. They express scant patience for a doctrine whose theory, they state, does not accord with the practice of current political systems. They even cast doubt on the participatory nature of the classical participatory ideal of fifth-century Athens. Robert Dahl goes so far as to brand advocates of participatory politics irrational in their quest for the unrealizable. He charges that "infantile fantasies" have gripped some of these believers in "magic."

These doubts relate quite directly to the political biases of the theorists in question, to concern with efficiency, to the pluralist skepticism about the degree of popular interest and information regarding politics, and to reservations about whether or not increased participation by the masses will bring with it irrationality and even totalitarianism.

Many primary democrats acknowledge these doubts, but they reject the idea that the present fears and alarms will necessarily make sense when a more participatory era develops. They believe that people must be given an opportunity to grow, and that when they are, they will blossom into responsible, aware, and intelligent citizens. Naturally, they appear ignorant and disinterested today, because they are not given a chance. Primary democrats say that by not moving to a politics in which there is a vastly expanded role for individual persons, we only reinforce the negative image of ordinary citizen—which may be real today—which pluralist democrats tell us and themselves is the truth. We have created a self-fulfilling prophecy.

A third and final element in the primary democrats' case is their argument that their democracy is open to change and is eager for an environment of growth and development. They claim that participatory democracy is confident in its assessment of human nature and ready for whatever alterations time and human enterprise bring. They contrast this confidence with what they take to be the narrow conservatism of pluralist democracy, a conservatism, they suggest, that focuses exclusively on the dangers of change and the glories of stability.

Pluralists respond by denying their critics' rigidly conservative image of them. They insist that they welcome change too, but only change that proceeds within an orderly and stable polity, which they doubt participatory democracy can provide. Moreover, they believe that primary democrats exaggerate the amount of change people seek. They suspect that most citizens like a largely familiar and secure environment. As a result, pluralists celebrate their theory of incremental change, one they contend speaks to the need for modest, ongoing change within a realm of assured stability.

Many of the warnings of pluralists critics of participatory democracy should not be ignored. They point to challenging practical difficulties, and their pessimism about human possibilities in politics requires respect. Yet participatory democrats are right to remind us that realism and pragmatism are not the only perspectives to apply in seeking what is right in political life. The question is not only what will "work." It is also what is right.

POPULISM

Another version of democracy is populism, a view held by many in the United States since the late nineteenth century. Populist democracy consists of a combination of active majoritarianism and a strong, decisive, central government. It is, in one sense, primary democracy that has made peace with efficiency. All populists agree that Western societies have fallen short of representing the majority will, despite their democratic rhetoric, especially in policy matters. They claim that pluralism has induced us to acquiesce in the ongoing surrender of government to political elites, special-interest groups, and political action committees (PACS) representing particular points of view. They urge that government return to the people who ought to rule in a democracy.

The ancestors of modern populists were the agrarian populists of almost a century ago, those American democrats who wanted governmental aid for their problems and who fondly, but incorrectly, believed that a majority in their nation agreed with their demands. They, like modern populists, identified assorted special interests that they asserted were consciously blocking change and therefore damaging democracy. Populists, among others, were zealous advocates of devices aimed to ensure a popular vote on major policies approved by legislatures (referenda). They also pressed for acceptance of laws to allow citizens to remove elected officials when the majority wanted them removed (recall). Many cities and states retain and occasionally use these populist measures, and a good number of modern populists would like to see them become more widespread. They assert that there is no other way to achieve a truly significant popular impact on government.

Populists make two important arguments on behalf of their democratic theory. First, they are confident that populism is at least as democratic as primary democracy and a good deal more so than pluralism. Populists earnestly hope to see the end of the day when "special interests" rule. They consider it ridiculous for pluralists to pretend they are democrats, since government by elites hardly constitutes democracy. On the other hand, they do agree that leadership is important, indeed indispensable, though they suggest that pluralist elites are scarcely kept in touch with the masses by an occasional election or two. Leaders must be approved frequently by the people, and their policies ratified by popular vote, in order for democratic legitimacy to exist.

Populists also seek to persuade us that only populist democracy cares about the broad public interest. In their opinion populist governors would naturally think in this framework, since they would be strictly accountable to the majority will. They see pluralism, on the other hand, as a system that encourages each citizen to think only of his or her selfish interest. While this judgment overlooks the pluralists who do focus on what they describe as the public interest, it is an accurate description of pluralists who contend that the results of competing interests and interest groups, as they appear in governmental decisions and nondecisions, *are* the public interest.

The second aspect of the populists' case is their conviction that populist democracy is a formula for action, for getting things done. In their minds, democracy does not connote delay, equivocation, or stalemate. As far as populists are concerned, pluralist democracy often fails to tackle difficult domestic problems. Established elites and special-interest groups have so many cozy vetoes over policy that it is hard for any new policy actions to take place. They charge that this is the reality in all too many pluralist settings, from the ineffective governments in such European countries as Italy to the United States, where the medical profession, oil companies, and others block change. Moreover, the same problem, they suspect, would overwhelm any participatory polity. It would be so decentralized and lack so much vital coordination that nothing much could be accomplished in terms of overall policy.

On the other hand, to their critics populists can sound a bit authoritarian. But populists believe that strong government authority need not end in despotism. They approve only a strong government closely responsive to public desires. Thus many populists attack the U.S. record in foreign affairs. There they see activism, but activism by an undemocratic leadership operating in an undemocratic manner. They ask who of us have ever approved our foreign policy.

Their argument for a democratic leadership does not, however, satisfy either participatory democrats or pluralists. Primary democrats doubt that populists can depend so much on leadership, while at the same time urging popular participation. They suspect that something will have to give and they expect it to be popular involvement. Their claim is that populists have begged the question in their critique of participatory democracy. The major point is not merely the size of the government, but whether there is direct public rule, which participatory democrats believe is most effective on as local a level as possible. Meanwhile, pluralists regard populist democracy as a danger to every minority. Not only do they foresee majority tyranny, but they fear it will be doubly dangerous since the majority will have a powerful centralized leadership at its command. They contend that democracy means majority rule reconciled with minority rights and they fear for the latter under populism.

Many social scientists also raise the objection that the populist talk about a majority will is no more than a romantic illusion. Ordinarily there is, they say, no majority will on which to build a democracy, only a series of temporary majority coalitions on specific issues and candidates that decay as fast as they develop in the shifting sands of public sentiment. They also contend that there is no obvious public interest; there are only varying (and passing) outlooks on what is the public interest.

DEMOCRATIC SOCIALISM

Within the United States there is no doubt that the debate over alternative forms of democracy takes place largely within the confines of pluralism, participatory democracy, and populism. In the larger world, however, another alternative, what we may term socialist democracy, receives much attention. The range of democratic socialism's appeal is great. Despite such imperfect examples as Sweden, it has proved popular as a rallying cry—more so than as a form of government.

Most democratic socialists identify four features in democracy, although how much they emphasize one or another can vary a good deal. First, they stress the importance of approximate economic equality among all citizens. Second, they argue that the entire community must own the major means of production, or at least have effective control over them. Third, they favor a good deal of participation by workers in key economic decisions—worker democracy. Finally, they insist that there can be no democracy unless citizens are roughly equal politically.

Three arguments socialist democrats make for their viewpoint are especially central. They always contend that democracy must be a way of life among people who respect each other as persons. From this angle only a democracy that creates and maintains citizens of approximately equal station in life (very much including economic life) can possibly instill such respect. According to this view, when equality does not exist, respect inevitably goes to the powerful and the moneyed, even if it is the respect of hate. Socialist democrats vigorously challenge other democrats: Isn't democracy about equal respect for the voice and wisdom of everyone? If it is, then we have to create an economic system that ensures equal respect in practice, not a standard that people ignore in practice.

Second, socialist democrats argue that democracy must be about a just life and a just society. It is not simply a method of decision making. It is, again, a way of life—that must never be forgotten. For socialist democrats this means that there is another reason for concern with rough economic equality for all citizens. It is what social justice demands. Although not all are Marxists, they usually follow Marx's definition of justice: to each according to his or her similar needs. Not to follow this goal, they think, is to deny respect for each human being.

Third, socialist democrats are convinced that such a democratic society— such a socialist democracy—is also valuable for a practical political reason. It will free citizens to participate as near equals in the decision-making processes of government. Socialist democrats find it absurd that the American political system—indeed, almost all political systems—claim to support democratic political equality, while actually allowing enormous economic inequalities, apparently on the assumption that one can separate the economic and political spheres. Socialist democrats deny this vigorously, declaring that the two realms are deeply and permanently intertwined. They believe that there can be considerable political equality only when there is substantial economic equality. Only when people see behind the fact that everyone has the vote in the United States, only when they note that it is the few who have and employ money in politics who really count in election campaigns—or even more in the interest-group process—will they abandon the illusion that pluralism is democracy. Then citizens will come to their senses and insist on much more economic equality as an essential prerequisite to democratic politics among equals.

The strong link between economic and political equality makes socialist democracy unique among democratic theories today. Except for an occasional participatory democrat or populist democrat who is also firmly committed to this kind of linkage, socialist democrats stand alone. This is also true of socialist democrats' contention that considerable public ownership and/or control of the economy is essential for democracy. In fact, this is what makes these democrats socialist democrats. The declining enthusiasm among some socialist democrats for public ownership of most of the economy (as opposed to control of it) is really peripheral to the essential point. Ownership or control, they expect the result to be the same: The economy will serve the general community and not act as the major source of human inequality.

It should be noted, finally, that socialist democrats do not have in mind a single form that democratic socialism should take. Usually they argue that this is an important, but secondary, question. Some favor a strong national government, elected by citizens in competitive free elections, while insisting that government must be bound by the goal of rough equality and considerable worker participation in the workplace far below the national government. Others favor a sharply decentralized political system in which the ideals of participatory democracy come true, but in a socialist setting that emphasizes worker self-management in the workplace.

Critics of socialist democracy abound. Pluralists lead the way, saying that it is one thing to favor equality of opportunity in political or economic life and quite another to force substantive equality. They do not think people will tolerate the latter, given a choice. Pluralists are not sure people will continue to have a choice under such a system. The truth about socialist democrats, these critics suggest, is that they have a low commitment to liberty. Despite socialist democrats' disclaimers that they want to protect political freedom to speak out, to petition, to run for office, pluralists are skeptical. They doubt that a society that is no longer very pluralistic in economic terms can provide enough independent groups with clout to block the excesses and errors of those in power.

Moreover, they suspect that most democratic socialists are so committed to their hatred for capitalism and the rich and their desire for economic equality that to achieve this goal they might sacrifice democratic liberties in the name of "economic democracy" or "the public good" or "temporary necessity." They cite a long list of revolutions that have occurred in the modern world under the broad rubric of democratic socialism. And they note that almost all soon abandoned democratic liberties and thus democracy. Pluralists fear there would be too much elite rule and far, far too little fragmented power—or pluralism.

The second argument pluralists make is that socialist democracy's demands for political and economic equality run directly against human nature, or at least human experience. This is not merely a matter of repeating contentions about the inevitable inequalities caused in politics by differences in interest, luck, or skills. It is also a question of the possibility of achieving anything like economic equality—and then maintaining it—as the basis for significant political equality. Pluralists look at the economic life of nations, from the United States to the Soviet Union. Official goals may differ, but the reality is sharp income differentials and a striving by a major sector of both populations to get more, economically, than others. There is little behavioral commitment to economic equality.

Populists and participatory democrats also make two main objections. First, they contend that the matter of the form of government is much more important than most socialist democrats think. Each understands that there is a stream of socialism closer to their particular view of the appropriate form—some socialists are more participatory, some more populist. Both insist that the direction socialist democracy takes when it sets up its political system will always have an enormous impact on whether it is democratic. Participatory democrats assert that any democratic socialism that does not concentrate largely on participation will be more socialism than democracy, something that is true of most socialist states today. Populists assert that ignoring the importance of leadership as well as participation will doom any socialist democracy to impotence. On the other hand, they criticize existing socialist regimes for failing to provide for participation and for seeing it as a threat to leadership.

Populists and participatory democrats are, second, predictably uncomfortable with the socialist aspect of democratic socialism. Most participatory enthusiasts, like many populists, are hardly eager devotees of giant corporations—or giant unions. They also usually recognize the gap in influence that sharp income differentials ensure. Since both theories of democracy are efforts to increase popular influence and to reduce the role of special interests whose roots are often in economic selfishness, there is a natural sympathy with socialist democracy.

Yet populists and participatory democrats usually think it is unnecessary to go to the "extreme" of socialism or socialist control of the economy. In part this is a dispute about how great the social changes need to be to expand democracy. In part it is a dispute over whether or not the economic factor is as overwhelming in human motivation as democratic socialists assert. There is a third element, too. For populists and many participatory democrats, there is considerable suspicion that socialists are more in love with economic equality and socialist control than with democracy. Participatory democrats and populists agree that if people in their political systems choose these goals, then they should be implemented. They often doubt, however, whether a socialist democracy would let a modified capitalism back if the people wanted it. Often the socialist democrat is confident that people would never take such a "reactionary" path, but who knows? Moreover, while socialist democrats insist that they have a strong commitment to civil liberties and political freedom, and argue that it is not fair to prejudge them on the basis of other, nondemocratic socialist regimes, their critics wonder what will happen in practice.

CONCLUSION

The many ideas and issues discussed in this chapter and the preceding one have a common theme: They concern controversies over what constitutes a legitimate polity in general and what particular institutional variant of it is the best. The concepts of legitimate and best as we have used them here are not abstractions. They refer to basic political values that can and should be maximized by political communities. It is the authors' belief that the value of human life is the most important one that politics ought to seek to maximize. As we will develop in subsequent chapters, many other values can be derived from this basic one, including—but not limited to—political equality, liberty, participation, and justice.

We argue that the state can be justified only if it allows people to relate to each other in a morally acceptable way—that is, if it recognizes the value of human life, and if its institutions and rules provide equality, liberty, and sufficient opportunity for its people to participate in the decisions that affect their lives. These and other parallel values must be assured before the state can earn their voluntary political obligation, through its deeds instead of through the use of coercive force. A good state, then, must allow human beings to develop their potential by serving their needs and desires to accommodate each other. A good state must never be an end in itself. It must be a means toward a good politics.

Democracy is the form of polity that best approximates that goal. As we have pointed out, democracy includes not solely the modern Western concept of a liberal representative system, but a broad variety of institutional arrangements and values, which can be assembled in different ways to form a polity that allows people to participate in political affairs to the extent that they can hold the state liable and responsive to their needs. We agree that too often discussions of democracy in the West focus exclusively on pluralism. This is one reason we have devoted so much effort to an examination of the competing claims of participatory democrats, populists, and socialist democrats. We might also have explored the views of those who see China and Cuba as valid democracies, or discussed the idea of British conservative thinkers, such as Michael Oakeshott, that tradition, representing the accumulation of human experience, is democracy at its best. But we think the debate among pluralists, populists, participatory democrats, and socialist democrats brings out important aspects of the enduring debate over the nature of democracy.

Democracy, conceived as the opportunity for regularized popular participation in public decision making, is the ideal (if not perfection) for human government. We acknowledge at the same time that it may come in many forms in theory and practice. It is not easy to state explicitly which of even those types is superior. In part, the choice will depend on the circumstances. One of the reasons for the historical variety of democratic regimes has been that large and small states, pastoral and industrial ones, and those with an educated versus an uneducated populace have had need for different types of democracy. The need for rapid political and economic development of so much of the Third World requires much more regimentation than is necessary in the postindustrial societies of today. The type of democracy possible and preferable will be unlikely to be the same for all.

Nevertheless, some generalizations are in order. The pluralists make their democratic theory too remote and too elite oriented—they do not make individual participation meaningful (which is different from regular) enough to be reliably responsive to public needs. Participatory democracy, thought of as radical decentralization, on the other hand, ignores the institutional framework that is necessary to solve regional, continental, and international problems like ecological policy and war, which encompass areas that are not confined to geographical and political boundaries. Populist democratic theory, too, has as a major flaw its naive assumptions about the nature of political problems. It allows only for episodic and spasmodic public participation in such things as referenda or recall, which does not make up for the elitist nature of most political institutions. What is more, it gives too little attention to problems of minorities in a polity.

In the final analysis, there is no perfect democratic government, or any other perfect government, for that matter. It is not really possible to have a great deal of leadership and action, rigorous control over rulers, and massive participation all in one democratic system. Participatory democracy is attractive because it does come closest to actual popular rule in principle, as would populism in the large societies in which we actually live. Pluralism offers the possibility of representing people in groups better than any other form of democracy and can provide the leadership societies need, but only if it exists in a reformed arrangement in which political opportunity is more equally shared than is often true in societies that claim to be pluralist today. Socialist democracy addresses the question of equal political opportunity, which is its main value in an exploration of democratic theory, and in its way raises disturbing questions for pluralists, populists, and even participatory democrats.

Our own inclinations go toward a form of democratic politics that stresses the importance of participation more than is the case with pluralist politics. Without citizen involvement there is reason to question the degree to which one has a democracy at all. Yet, as we have noted, there are problems with all the alternatives to pluralism, as with any democratic theory. In the concrete case of the United States the answer does not lie in some other category of democracy. Perhaps we would do better to ask of our neopluralist democracy whether it might benefit from taking more seriously the concerns other democratic theories raise. We should ask whether there really is enough effort to facilitate popular participation in pluralism, a query that both the participatory democrats and the populists would raise. We should also ask whether there is enough emphasis on political equality, a question that social democrats would ask. We see both questions as challenges, and when applied to the theory and practice of democracy in the United States, disturbing ones. We think committed democrats cannot avoid facing them. Nor should they want to.

SUGGESTIONS FOR SUPPLEMENTARY READING

Berry, Jeffrey. *The Interest Group Society.* Boston: Little, Brown, 1984.

Cook, T. and P. Morgan, Eds. *Participatory Democracy.* San Francisco: Canfield, 1971.

Dahl, Robert. *After the Revolution?* New Haven: Yale University Press, 1971.

————. *Pluralist Democracy in the United States.* New York: Rand McNally, 1964.

Edelman, Murray. *Symbolic Uses of Politics.* Champaign: University of Illinois Press, 1964.

Eisinger, Peter. "Community Control and Liberal Dilemmas," *Publius,* (Fall 1972): 129–148.

Harris, Fred. *The New Populism.* New York: Saturday Review Press, 1976.

Heilbroner, Robert. *An Inquiry Into the Human Prospect.* New York: Norton, 1974.

Kariel, Henry, Ed. *Frontiers of Democratic Theory.* New York: Random House, 1970.

Margolis, Michael. *Viable Democracy.* New York: Penguin, 1979.

Mayo, Henry. *An Introduction to Democratic Theory.* New York: Oxford University Press, 1960.

Mill, John Stuart. *Utilitarianism, Liberty and Representative Government.* New York: Dutton, 1951.

Pateman, Carole. *Participation and Democratic Theory.* Cambridge: Cambridge University Press, 1970.

Sartori, Giovanni. *Democratic Theory.* New York: Praeger, 1967.

Spitz, Elaine. *Majority Rule.* Chatham, New Jersey: Chatham House, 1984.

Thompson, Dennis. *The Democratic Citizen*. Cambridge: Cambridge University Press, 1970.

Truman, David. *The Governmental Process*. New York: Knopf, 1951.

Wilson, Graham. *Interest Groups in the United States*. New York: Oxford University Press, 1981.

Wolff, R. P. *In Defense of Anarchy*. New York: Harper & Row, 1970.

4
Liberty and Equality—I

Cries for liberty and equality have resounded throughout history. They have built constitutions and overturned governments. They have etched themselves into the fabric of our political theories. They splash across the front pages of our daily newspapers. Patrick Henry's resistance to British rule was voiced in the cry "Give me liberty or give me death!" Jefferson wrote, "The tree of liberty must be watered by the blood of tyrants!" During the French Revolution the Parisian masses chanted "Liberty! Equality! Fraternity!" The English political theorist John Stuart Mill published a classic essay on the question of liberty. Rousseau, the apostle of community, wrote a discourse on the origins of inequality. In our own age the cries for liberty and equality resound even more loudly. Feminists demand equality, constitutionally and at the workplace, as well as at the political nominating convention. Libertarians and Reaganites attack the welfare state and its bureaucracy. Racial minorities seek equal treatment and a new place in the corridors of power. Reformers call for maintaining or creating standards of equality for homosexuals, prisoners, and mental patients. And there are backlashes in each of these areas from those who find their privileges being eroded or even extinguished.

In this and the following chapter we pursue the topics of liberty and equality. We consider them separately, but we also endeavor to discuss them in relationship to each other. Liberty and equality are as closely linked as any two political values we might name and, in fact, are so intimately intertwined that many theorists view them as being in balance—as one is advanced the other must be diminished. Theorists from Alexis de Tocqueville to John Stuart Mill, from Jean Jacques Rousseau to Albert Camus, have discussed them comparatively. We agree with these thinkers that it makes sense to view liberty and equality side by side, because such comparative analysis fosters an understanding of the nature and limitations of these interdependent political values.

To illustrate the depth of the interrelationship of liberty and equality, some examples are appropriate. Our first is familiar and has generated a great deal of controversy in many communities in recent years. It concerns the sale of a house. From the perspective of homeowners, it seems fair that those who pay for a house should have the freedom to sell that house to whomever they want. If they refuse to sell to someone of a different color, they feel justified in claiming it is nobody else's business. Let us, however, look at the same situation from the perspective of potential buyers who are of a different race than the seller. Perhaps such buyers have been victims of racial discrimination all of their lives. They have been forced to live in poor neighborhoods, send their children to substandard schools, put up with inferior municipal services, run increased risks of crime, and suffer all of the indignities ghetto dwellers are acquainted with. They want to buy a house and have made enough money to afford it. They feel that it is their right as human beings to live wherever they choose, as long as they can pay for it. They are advancing a claim that the liberties of a seller do not extend so far as to permit denial of their right to equal treatment.

Both claims, liberty and equality, have been advanced by the two parties in this kind of situation, and neither claim can be rejected out of hand as being totally invalid. The problem is not only that the "twin values" arise together with great frequency but that the claims of both are often mutually exclusive. If we grant the claims of one, those of the other party are denied.

The same thing is true of the longtime fight over inheritance laws. Many people object to steep inheritance taxes, arguing that there could be no more basic liberty than the right to make provision for one's children. Others contend that equality demands that everyone have an equal chance in life. Yet how can they, if the wealthy few are able to give their children the enormous advantage that we all know inherited wealth provides? Or consider a factory or utility owner, who maintains that he should have the liberty to produce his products in the freest possible manner, being confronted by a government demanding that equal rights of all to a clean environment require him to install costly antipollution devices. Is that not the very heart of the acid rain issue? The pollution control and safety accessories mandated by the government for our cars constitute a similar example. Buyers may feel it is their lungs and their life and that they should be free to choose whether to have those extra-cost devices. After all, it is their right as consumers to decide what to buy. On the other hand, the government has advanced a claim by the majority that equal access on the part of all citizens to a livable environment and an equal chance not to be smashed into by some out-of-control, death-trap car should take precedence over any consumer liberties. It is the very epitome of providing for the public interest.

All of these claims and counterclaims involve serious cases of conflicting liberties and equalities. What is needed is a thorough examination of the definitions and issues involved with liberty and equality, starting with consideration of each concept separately. We begin with liberty.

We tend to associate liberty with choice, specifically with ability to make choices. We commonly assume we are freest when we can choose to do what we will, when we are, so to speak, at liberty to do what we want. Freedom in this basic sense is not a thing we somehow possess, but a condition in which a person lives. Some conditions or situations are free because we can choose in them, others are not because one cannot make any choices.

Liberty/Freedom

A proper understanding of what freedom entails is actually a good deal more complicated, especially in a political context, but this analysis immediately raises a primary problem that we must face, even though we cannot solve it. Some thinkers, such as the contemporary psychologist B. F. Skinner,[1] argue that we cannot consider any form of liberty because there is no such thing—liberty is an illusion and, therefore, a nonexistent value. We begin our exploration of liberty by asking that most basic of questions: Can it really exist at all outside of our imaginations? Determinists, those who feel that we are not free, believe that our actions are completely fixed by heredity, the will of God, environment, and other forces beyond our control. If such a full determinist position is accepted, we are not free, by definition. In fact, it makes no sense to value liberty at all, since we are not responsible for any of our actions, all of which are mapped out for us and are beyond our ability to control.

On the other hand, there are many advocates of the concept that people do have, or can have, considerable liberty. Most political philosophers and many theologians have agreed that there are areas in which individuals can and do make choices that are not predetermined. No two thinkers, no two of us, are likely to agree on how expansive the realm of potential free choice is, or ought to be, for any of us. Some thinkers today, impressed by the factors of environment and heredity, edge close to the position of Skinner, while others remain confident that humans have an enormous capacity to make determinations for themselves as autonomous beings exercising free choice.

We do not dishonor a long and still lively tradition of philosophic discourse on the question of determinism and freedom, when we argue that the debate seems to us to have an air of unreality about it. We recognize that our conclusion is not universally shared, but we tend to think the question is one that cannot be resolved short of a position of faith. Evidence for each side usually turns out to be disappointingly lacking in conclusive proof.[2] Consequently, since we cannot find a definitive answer to the question of whether we are really free in a metaphysical sense, or whether it makes sense to talk of "genuine" liberty, we leave the question by concluding that it does not lead us anywhere for our purposes, interesting though it can be.

We start instead by assuming that we do have some choice in our lives. We make this particular assumption, because we think it is intrinsic to our entire aspiration for humanity, and because we respect the Western image of the humanistic individual, one capable of independent action, rational judgment, and genuine responsibility. This image of the human person is crucial for our understanding of political morality. Our political theories and our whole ethical thought builds on a concept of an individual who can often choose and often is responsible for his actions.[3] Indeed, if we cannot choose and are never responsible, then there is no point in considerations of what we ought to do in personal morality or in politics.

Yet we appreciate that liberty is always constrained by natural and environmental factors. At one extreme are factors generic to our human species that inevitably limit our potential liberty. This reality is obvious and yet worth considering for a moment. Human beings cannot fly without benefit of airplanes or similar aids, and they cannot be in two places at once. We cannot swim rivers like a fish or outrun our game animals. The list of things we cannot do is almost endless; in fact, it would be much easier to list the things we can do. The natural restraints on our liberty are important, because they define the limits to our potential freedom. It makes no difference to us if there is nobody to stop us from soaring like an eagle; we cannot, and therefore can never have any meaningful liberty to do so.

Many hereditary or developmental features circumscribe many choices in every person's unique life. Despite modern medicine, none of us can choose to live forever, or to become children again. Few who are ugly can become beautiful, fewer yet who have no athletic skill can become great athletes, and none at all who have low intelligence can have the meaningful liberty to become great intellects.

We suffer substantial limitations as a result of environmental background as well. Obviously, our personal experiences in growing up and in dealing with life's pressures mold and shape us, sometimes in ways we cannot easily overcome, and thereby limit our potential liberty. Moreover, citizens of a rich country are likely to have substantially more choices available to them than are those of poor nations, just as a suburban child with upper-middle-class parents is likely to have more real freedoms than the average ghetto child.

Environmental limitations are far more controversial than are the factors of nature or heredity. How much are our choices limited by our background? Consider the classic example of the fight over welfare policies. Some contend that many people on welfare are not trapped by their personal and situational environment so much as by their laziness and unwillingness to get out and work. This viewpoint does not consider environmental determinism very strong in this case. Others insist that many on welfare are indeed locked into a situation, a culture of poverty, which they are helpless to rectify. Such an opinion reveals considerable belief in environmental determinism. Statistics offered for one case or the other make no impact on the argument, because their significance is interpreted according to one's general beliefs more than by any objective reality.

We do not think that any easy answers are forthcoming to the question of the influence one's background may exercise in delimiting choices. It seems to us that there is no profit in following either the persuasion of those who dismiss the effects of the environment or those who are overwhelmingly impressed with its chains. Both perspectives are far too sweeping for the detailed and complicated reality of human experience. We are inclined to say that the amount of potential freedom one may have will vary from one environmental situation to another. Only by examining concrete people and environments can one speak with much confidence about the degree of liberty that is actually available.

Such a process requires that we look not only at the effect of our personal and cultural background but as well at specific moments of choice and the environmental constraints they may impose. One intriguing manner of thinking about this feature of the problem is evident in the recent work of Alan Wertheimer. His view is that even when we agree that people have the potential for liberty of choice in a specific situation, they still may not be free in any but a meaningless formal sense.

Wertheimer's insight builds on the undeniable fact that choices have consequences. Sometimes the consequences will be favorable and sometimes not. When, however, the costs of a choice involve serious deprivations for the person making the choice, it is likely that that choice will not be made, even though it is not prevented by the person's heredity or background, even though that person is technically free to make it. We can, in fact, predict that when negative consequences are perceived to be great for choosing to do X, most people will not do so, hence Wertheimer's term "predictive freedom." The exact test that Wertheimer suggests we should use he formulates as follows: "We want to say that A is unfree . . . to do X when the likelihood and severity of a deprivation make it unreasonable to expect A to do X." The obvious implication is that even when we appear to be free we often cannot fairly be considered so.[4]

Does all of this mean that we can never be free? Pervasive as these limitations may be, beyond them lies an arena of human personal, social, and political experiences. Luckily, the possibilities of action in this arena are so vast that they could easily keep us busy for millennia without there being any danger of exhausting the frontiers of human experience. We still have open a wide range of life-styles, values, and possible political communities. These more than make up for the tangled web of physical limitations, regulations, and cultural patterns that foster pessimism. These days, even the sky is not the limit.

However much liberty we may have potentially, our use of any of it immediately leads us to the realm of moral life and social and political philosophy. Those who live alone—hermits—have no need for any concept of liberty other than that which they can observe in nature. They can do what they please, unmolested by others; they bother and affect no one by their behavior. Hence, their liberty is devoid of moral implication. But most of us are not hermits and do not wish to be. We live our lives in a permanent state of interaction with others. Political communities are places of close social proximity; what we do in them has a reciprocal effect—our actions affect other citizens and theirs affect us. Thus, our freedoms in a polity do have moral implications, because of the inseparability of our mutual needs and wants. Our liberty and what we do with it is a subject of moral concern, because it influences the quality of life and other political values. In short, while liberty may be abstract as a general concept, in a political community it becomes a moral reality. As such, its meanings and interaction with other values are the proper subject of political theory, which deals with moral evaluation and prescription about collective relationships.

Although liberty as a political value has been postulated in literally hundreds of different ways, there are three concepts that are central to the debate about the subject. At one end of the spectrum lies the view of those who advocate the greatest liberty and consequently have an individualistic focus to their prescriptions. At the other end is the concept of those who insist that relatively little liberty is desirable—those who are, therefore, advocates of restricting individual freedoms in the interests of the whole political community. Those who prescribe less liberty than the individualists but more than the collectivists fall into a middle position. They seek a balance between the individual and the community, and equilibrium between the interests of the one and the other.

NEGATIVE FREEDOM AND INDIVIDUAL RIGHTS

At one extreme of our continuum are those who put great emphasis on freedom, particularly for individuals. They believe that individual liberty is of such great importance that it should take precedence over collective interests. As they understand liberty, it is the greatest possible opportunity to make as many choices as possible, a situation that imposes the fewest possible exterior restrictions upon an individual. They often believe that a polity cannot restrict any important rights of the individual. Their focus has been on what is usually called negative freedom. That is, they look at freedom as something that is threatened by environmental forces, most often by the state, and that must be protected at all times by vigilance. The term "negative freedom" invokes the idea that freedom must be preserved by negating the elements that are constantly seeking to diminish it. For them the battle for freedom is a negative battle in that it involves fighting off these forces, particularly the government. Thus they have always sought to erect barriers of "rights" around people's liberties to keep unwanted interferences at bay.

The Case for the Negative-Freedom Approach

Negative freedom is the classic doctrine of the great liberal theorists, beginning in the seventeenth century with Hobbes and Locke. They understood human beings in a framework that saw them as naturally free, as naturally able to make choices without much restriction. But they also did not think people were capable of getting on well with each other without some government, without some checks on unbridled liberty. Hence, they believed that government was formed to check the few or the many who abuse others in pursuit of their self-interest. The true aim of government was to realize as much liberty as possible and to protect as many rights as possible. Yet government was a danger and often had proven to be so. Liberty could be threatened and often was by governments that went beyond their minimum functions of providing order for liberty. The signers of the Declaration of Independence had just this concept of negative liberty. For them the British government had exceeded its task of providing a safe environment for the use of liberties. It had to be thrown off, because it repeatedly transgressed against basic liberties that people had a natural right to exercise. This attitude, of course, continues in our era in the so-called conservative wing of U.S. politics.

The term "right" is a very important one. A right is an absolute that cannot be denied by any person or authority. Natural rights are something all individuals possess in their very personhood and not from any particular rank or status, though there are specific status-oriented rights that some theorists recognize. Certain privileges are part of being human—they are inexorably natural—and transcend human societies or preferences.

There are several categories of commonly asserted rights. One of these is the right of religious freedom. It is usually claimed to be a natural right and is often a protected legal right. As expressed in the U.S. Constitution (which is a fairly typical statement), this right guarantees freedom from religious persecution and freedom to practice whatever religion one believes. It guarantees the right to claim even that no God exists. It does not guarantee the right of a particular religion to use the laws of the state to compel obedience to its doctrines or practices, as Khomeini is doing in Iran and as a few extreme religious fundamentalists want in the United States.

Religious-freedom rights have a long history. People have long been persecuted, tortured, or killed in the name of religious absolutism, and in places like Northern Ireland and the Middle East religious hatred enters into the political controversies that divide people and governments today. Many liberal theorists conclude that the only way to avoid such religious disputes is to prevent any religious group or sect from gaining control of the state, by guaranteeing freedom of worship to all theological persuasions, no matter how bizarre or unpopular, as long as this is congruent with public safety. This pragmatic permission is important in itself; however, religious rights are extremely important to the liberal tradition, because of a widespread belief that they reflect the pervasive religiosity of mankind and the sacrosanct nature of free religious expression.

Another related category of rights that many often affirm may be called the rights of conscience. Although Henry Thoreau's and Martin Luther King, Jr.'s, writings[5] are the examples most familiar to contemporary American students, Europeans like John Stuart Mill and Alexis de Tocqueville[6] were prominent advocates of this right as well. Proponents of a right to conscience assert that individuals should be allowed to follow the dictates of their own carefully considered ideas about morality and that no person or group, public or private, should interfere. Indeed, they agree that individuals must be allowed to follow their own consciences, even when they conflict with commands from a political community to fight in what they consider immoral wars or to commit genocide or to change their individual tastes, styles, and beliefs of living.

It makes no difference to them whether the source of an unjust command is a dictator acting alone or the pressure of tens of millions of neighbors and fellow citizens; if one is commanded to do evil, the result is tyranny. As Leonard Hobhouse puts it; "liberty is no mere formula of law or the restriction of law. There may be a tyranny of custom, a tyranny of opinion, even a tyranny of circumstance, as real as any tyranny of government and more pervasive."[7]

John Stuart Mill was so insistent, in fact, that he claimed the right of individual freedom of conscience was absolute—no government or majority could restrict it at all, save only in the rare circumstances where its exercise would harm others. De Tocqueville warned about the dangers of a majoritarian tyranny in early American society that would erase individual liberties. Thoreau, too, was famous for the justification of his resistance against the laws that supported the slavery that he strongly opposed. He felt that it was a citizen's duty to employ his right of conscience by disobeying laws and governments that persisted in support of the immorality of slavery. Vietnam War resisters evoked similar claims, as do some advocates of Christian schooling.

While this right has been invoked by some noble people in just causes, it has problems that cannot be glossed over lightly. The principal problem is the source of the right itself, the conscience. Some people describe conscience as the sum total of one's moral values, derived through the socializing influences of relatives, schools, friends, churches, and so on. It is not, under this reading, anything more than an expression of one's environment, and scarcely to be trusted as a statement of eternal or, indeed, any morality. Still others suspect that too often what is called conscience is merely a fancy name for one's more or less spontaneous whims, or that beneath its imposing traditional moral grandeur may frequently be found shrewd self-interest. Others, of course, believe that we have a moral sense or, through reason and intuition, access to a moral standard, represented in our conscience, which quite transcends our environment, our whims, or our self-interest. This indeed was the whole point of Martin Luther King, Jr.'s, campaigns for change through nonviolent action. The stubborn suffering involved was intended as a mechanism to awaken in all white people their consciences, to activate the truth in all of us.

No matter which interpretation one agrees with, it is nonetheless fair to warn that the right to conscience must be investigated in every case with some carefulness. While it is reasonable to respect the rights of conscience and to be guided by conscience, we need to remember that some who pursue the rights of conscience are doing no more than attempting to imbue their belief with a mystical or sacrosanct aura that covers over what are strictly personal opinions, no matter how sincerely held. Moreover, those who appeal to conscience tend to assume that their conscience is automatically right, no matter what it tells them, as well as that one who invokes it has an absolute right to follow it no matter what the political implications may be. We do not agree that it is automatically sacred and it is our position that a right of conscience is valid, not when its "truth" is proclaimed but only when its source is probed and its dictates are conscientiously prescribed, argued, and justified as to their moral worth. It is quite irrational to invoke the right of conscience as the only rationale for a sweeping political position, if that position is not justifiable by reasoned moral argumentation as well.

We must face the fact that consciences vary extensively. People on each side of most conflicts have claimed that their consciences compelled their actions. Perhaps they did, but simple assertions of rights based on conscience do not always make very convincing moral cases and certainly offer no acceptable proof. Advocates of rights to conscience, like Thoreau or some modern terrorists, often do not feel obligated to give adequate and detailed rationales for their positions of conscience that they have elevated to sanctity. They claim that their moral position is consistent with "the laws of nature," "right reason," or "divine revelation." People either see truth or they do not. Conscience advocates often claim that there is no need to explain or justify "the laws of nature" to those who cannot comprehend them because they are defective in reasoning ability. Such claims cannot be refuted, because they do not rest on verifiable argumentation. For the same reason they cannot be accepted.

There are other problems with conscience, especially if it is held to be an unlimited right. A mere whim or the result of temporarily clouded reasoning powers may be mistaken for conscience. Such a mistake is fraught with great political consequences. General resistance to and absolute denial of majorities are serious and often irreversible actions that should not be undertaken on a whim that might later be contradicted by a fully awakened conscience. Furthermore, the absolute right of conscience has serious anarchic implications. If every individual is permitted to nullify the values and policies of the political community according to the dictates of conscience, there cannot be a political community. There are morally valid reasons for resistance in some situations (see Chapter 8 on authority and revolt), but advocates of an unlimited right to conscience go far beyond any theory of authority and revolt that recognizes the value of political communities.

Conversely, conscience must be respected as a stance when it is invoked to sustain the moral claims of individuals against statist or social values and demands that compel repugnant behavior. No one should have the right to force people to violate their deepest moralities. If, however, conscience rights are claimed in this context, they are subject to the same evaluation as any other claim of political morality. They have no automatic supremacy.

We should not reject rights of conscience out of hand, but we should be aware of the absolutist and the specious nature of some claims frequently advanced. Mill is correct when he asserts that people have private and public rights to pursue their own needs and desires as long as they do not directly hurt others by doing so, thereby claiming an importance for liberty that extends it up to the frontiers of basic equality. There is, however, no substitute for a commitment to moral reasoning, if we are to respect other people. This point is recognized by some of the activists who believe in conscience-informed civil disobedience. They make a careful effort to explain the reason for their actions and seek to convert others to their belief. This was the policy advocated by Martin Luther King, Jr., and it is the method practiced by many Quakers and others in the antinuclear movement today, especially groups like The Union of Concerned Scientists and Physicians for Social Responsibility.

Another alleged right, one of the most controversial, is the right to own and use private property. Property! The very word brings out some of the most intense passion and bitter arguments among human beings. There are many versions or degrees of this right, or liberty, to own property that different thinkers have defended over its long history. Some theorists have upheld the right to own property, subject to a number of restrictions imposed by the general political community. Others have had a much more sweeping concept of the property right, seeing it as virtually limitless. Certainly it has played an important part in Western political thought, especially since the rise of capitalism, and its most vigorous and sweeping advocates have been the so-called laissez-faire liberals.[8]

Although many theorists have set forth the concept of laissez faire, the most readable and understandable is the eighteenth-century Briton John Locke.[9] Locke sought to secure the rights of a property-owning class against both kings and commoners. In the present era such thinkers as Milton Friedman, the University of Chicago economist and Nobel laureate,[10] and William F. Buckley of television and newspaper fame, seek to carry on much of the laissez-faire tradition. They have the enthusiastic support of many millions of Americans.

Laissez faire, literal French for "allow to do," is understood by its advocates to mean that property rights, the acquisition, use, and social implications of material goods, and the power of capital are inviolable and should not be tampered with by any alleged public interest. While its origins go back to the idea of social contract,[11] advanced by property owners against the claims of divine-right kings, and have been used to secure property from restrictions, it reached its zenith with the rise of capitalism, which resulted from the Industrial Revolution. Supporters of laissez faire used the doctrine to justify their accumulation and exploitation of vast amounts of property, not just in land but in factories and the fruits of production made possible by and necessary for the Industrial Revolution. Capitalists employed their property rights to achieve virtually absolute control over the livelihood of millions of workers. The doctrine was used as a justification for industrialists' opposition to child-labor-regulation laws, wage-and-hour laws, and environmental controls of industry that would prevent the contamination of natural resources, and it was made into a successful defense against critics of the social ills caused by the Industrial Revolution that allowed the "robber barons" of Europe and America to build great industrial and financial empires with the labor of ordinary citizens. Economist Arthur Laffer, the guru of "supply-side economics," leads a chorus of similar claims today, though he and his followers accept more social regulations than their laissez-faire ancestors.

Though the use of a broad laissez-faire concept of the right to property as a barrier against social regulation is still with us, it is gradually giving way to a grudging recognition that rights of property are not inviolate and that we must consider how others are affected by the uses of property. Today the danger of the concept of an absolute right to property remains the fact that it can permit private accumulations of power that rival and even surpass governmental authorities, as witness the power and resources of our multinational corporations like International Telephone and Telegraph and Exxon to plot political revolutions or evade national regulation by moving headquarters and subsidiaries across borders.

There is also the problem of equality (see Chapter 6 on justice). It may be fair to give everyone an equal right to unrestricted acquisition and control of property, if there is an unlimited amount of property and if all people are equally equipped to get and hold it. The Industrial Revolution, however, was responsible for the permanent disappearance of those conditions, if they ever did exist. People do not start out in life equally—they are differentially equipped with wealth, social advantages, family connections, accidents of birth like race, and many other factors. Thus, some start with a tremendous advantage in their ability to monopolize goods and power. As on a track used for running foot races, those who have the inside lane will win every time (assuming roughly equal running speeds), because that lane is shorter. "Justice" in modern track and field events dictates that the starting point be staggered, insuring real and not alleged equality of opportunity to win the race. So it is with unrestricted property rights. They are unjust, because the claimed liberty for all to have the right to property does not exist in a stratified society with finite resources.

This does not mean that all property rights are ridiculous or automatically unjust. Some of them continue to make sense. History shows us that the laissez-faire bulwarks against royal claims on the property of nonroyal classes gradually lost urgency as conditions changed. Today the question has evolved into whether unrestricted property rights supply a satisfactory public atmosphere. Most contemporary Western thinkers, particularly Europeans, do not ignore or dismiss the right to property altogether, but most do not think about it as an unrestricted right. Instead, they talk of the right to property as one right among a number, with which it will not always harmonize. They visualize a complex balance of many rights, including property rights, with the general aim of trying to achieve the largest social benefit. This objective necessarily involves restrictions on property rights and, for some thinkers, drastic limitations on such rights, as well as enforcement of these limitations by public authorities.

Another group of rights with which we are all familiar today are the rights to free speech, free press, and assembly. These basic political rights are, like the others, often derived from natural laws, but as often today are based on the utilitarian argument that they are essential to the achievement of a satisfactory form of human self-government. No rights are more familiar to the American tradition of politics and none have been more honored (in theory, and often in practice) in American history. But even these rights are rarely held to be absolute in constitutional practice. There are limitations to what can be said (incitement to riot), what can be printed (libel), and what kinds of meetings may be held (a meeting to plan treason) that few theorists of these basic rights dispute.

The First Amendment to the U. S. Constitution, which provides for these rights, is an almost classic case of the negative-freedom philosophy in writing, for it provides that "Congress shall make no law" to block these rights. The image it forms is one that suggests that rights are possessions that must be protected against government above all and that are in constant danger, a doctrine that liberals and American conservatives for centuries have held to be self-evident and inescapable.

A final group of rights that have been important to those who advocate negative freedom are a broad class of procedural privileges. These rights are the basic philosophical underpinnings of the due-process clause of the U.S. Constitution and are widely recognized in most Western governmental and private organizations. This basis of the Western judicial system, with its roots deep in England's common-law heritage, was intimately associated with the demands of property owners in preindustrial times that their property not be taken through taxation or otherwise without a series of fair hearings and appeals. It was, and continues to be, advanced by the accused and by defenders of the unpopular, who wish to protect themselves from arbitary and/or bigoted actions by governmental officials. Champions of procedural rights ask that every person subject to criminal prosecution, job dismissal, and other circumstances of personal jeopardy or denial of rights be entitled to a fair and open hearing. Included are rights to confront and question accusers, rights to expert counsel, rights to jury trials in criminal cases, and many other due-process procedures. We consider this further in the chapter on justice.

Procedure is a necessary but not sufficient safeguard of individual and community interests. But the faith that some liberals have that securing procedural rights for all will automatically result in just outcomes is naive.[12] They are correct in their claim that if procedures are so rigged that one side is automatically favored, hearings are going to be shams. Even the best procedures followed in the service of poor, discriminatory, or arbitrary laws and regulations cannot guarantee fairness. Surely defendants are convicted unjustly, even if due process is followed, if they are members of unpopular minorities or espouse very unpopular causes. Thus, justice goes well beyond procedure. Those who have faith in an "invisible hand" of due process should look to more reliable tenets of political morality, if they are to be sure of justice being done.[13] In the final analysis, justice as merely due process is insufficient.

This critical analysis of rights is not meant to be exhaustive, of course. There are other rights held by serious thinkers (such as the right to life or the right to economic security) that can profitably be analyzed as well. This list simply illustrates the points sufficiently to put the concept into perspective for the beginning student by covering the major areas.

Problems With the Negative-Liberty Approach

There are several difficulties with an approach to freedom that proceeds through negative liberty. First, one has to be clear where the source of liberty is. Very often arguments on this subject, like vague appeals for "human rights" in international politics, consist of little more than a claim for a liberty without an explanation regarding what the ultimate grounding of this liberty is. We have seen that in the Western tradition this source is very often natural rights. If this is the position, there are further matters that require attention before giving it our automatic acceptance. We have argued that merely asserting the existence of a natural right is of no particular help to anyone, nor is it especially convincing. Those who claim natural rights must make some effort to explain how they have obtained knowledge of this natural truth. Contrary to Jefferson and the Declaration of Independence, rights are not self-evident or obvious, and they cannot be sustained by this method alone. A careful and conscientious effort must be made to demonstrate as best one can that such rights are basic to what it means to be human, are basic to what is natural for human beings. It often helps to demonstrate that one's concept of a right has been held by other thinkers of the past, not because this appeal to authority automatically proves anything, but because it allays the reasonable fear that the claim of a natural right for this or that liberty, being difficult to disprove, may be used as a quick defense when all else fails.

Second, if one employs a natural-rights basis for liberty or anything else, it is important to be clear about just what that natural right encompasses. A right to liberty is no more than a vague abstraction that includes everything and thus nothing. Liberties are specific: the right to freedom of speech, the right to freedom of the press, and so on—not the right to "freedom." The curses of political theory are vagueness and grand abstractions that no one really means and that no one can really understand.

Third, excessive reliance on a natural-rights basis for liberty often avoids the hard question of the relations between one or another kind of liberty and the social and political order at large. A natural-rights basis for liberties often is an intensely individualistic approach, and its implications should, at the least, be pondered; for the natural-rights approach views liberties as the domain of each and every individual against all else and all others. It proclaims the individual as supreme over all else. How far do we want to carry this doctrine? Moreover, we should ask ourselves about the social basis for rights. Whether or not we think that the basic liberties we favor are natural in their origin, it is a fact that political communities are the context in which they are fulfilled and, indeed, the context in which they are often denied. We must not ignore our roles and lives in the broader social life of a political community by ceaselessly talking in terms of natural rights. As political animals, proximity to others is a reality.

Ultimately the question is whether or not the Western tradition of thinking about liberty in terms of negative liberty is useful. Modern analytic philosophers—those who think about our language in making political arguments—raise serious doubts on this issue. Perhaps the most exciting and most challenging recent attack on negative liberty as a way to understand the nature of freedom has come from the political philosopher Gerald MacCallum.[14] He argues that when political theorists in the Western tradition talk of liberty, they speak too much as if it were a possession that exists only by the removal of another force that blocks its exercise. In other words, they talk of negative liberty.

In fact, MacCallum's analysis of ordinary language shows that when we speak of freedom, what we really say is that we want to be "free from" something (the language of those who are in the negative-liberty tradition) in order to be "free to" do something. We never have in mind general abstractions, like freedom conceived as the absence of all restraint, or anything of the sort. Instead, we are interested in removing a specific blockage in order to accomplish, or have the opportunity to accomplish, a specific positive action. Liberty is not, as many who are sympathetic to negative liberty imagine, a possession that we want to hold inviolate forever, but an instrument that we want to use for specific purposes. With this understanding, we should talk less of the natural right to liberty and more, for instance, of the right to free speech, undeterred by the government, for the purpose of making our voices heard in the political system. And, indeed, MacCallum argues convincingly, this is exactly what we do in practice. The enormous advantage of his linguistic discovery is that it allows arguments in political theory to move from sweeping assertions about liberty in general to specific liberties, limitations, and purposes for which a liberty is to be exercised. On these matters meaningful arguments can be made, and liberty can return from the realm of vague rhetoric to the arena of concrete argument in a manner that makes policy judgments more sensible.

POSITIVE FREEDOM AND THE CONCEPT OF THE ORGANIC COMMUNITY

Political thinkers who believe in the concept of positive freedom are at the opposite pole of our continuum of positions on liberty. As negative freedom envisions a very small (negative) role for the state in the lives of citizens and concentrates on rights that protect individuals against collective claims, so positive freedom as an opposing approach envisions the political community playing an active (positive) role in the lives of citizens and puts a greater premium on collective privileges and interest then it does on individual rights. Exponents of this perspective have included such classical giants as Plato[15] and Aristotle and such modern thinkers as Hegel, Marx, and Rousseau.[16]

The Case for Positive Freedom

These political theorists insist that we are not self-contained centers of consciousness and being. As biological organisms we might be able to survive alone under favorable conditions, but we take on our "true" humanity only as components or organs in a collectivity such as the Greek city-state, the General Will of Rousseau, or the classless society that Marx hints at. By their lights, each person is an interdependent component of the whole community, which, like a living organism, is a satisfying collectivity that is greater than the simple sum of each of the components.[17] The community is both the product and the ultimate definer of each of its members. As a natural organism, it receives its "life" from the contributions of each part; it also gives meaningful life to each member. The citizens of the organism (political community) cannot live outside of the larger body and vice versa.

Thus, the organic polity exists because of the interactions of each of its citizens, who are no longer solitary human animals because of their participation in a meaningful whole.

Organic theorists define liberty as a political value in a way that is quite different from the familiar negative-liberty perspective. To them, liberty by definition is the result of participation in a political collectivity. Many of these theorists, especially Hegel and Plato, felt that genuine freedom was not the individual liberties that advocates of personal rights imagine. They contend that that leads to a ceaseless competition or, even worse, a solitary atomism that cuts people off from meaningful human and political interaction. Instead, genuine freedom is the increased opportunities and satisfactions that are the result of the civilized political life that only an organic community can supply. These options of virtue, comfort, and interpersonal relationships that allow all parties to prosper spiritually and materially are truly the liberation of the human potential—what frees people to be "genuinely human." Thus, advocates contend, while those who can do as they please are technically free, in reality they have no fellow citizens and mutual institutions to make liberty meaningful.

This position is not quite the same as a strand of Western liberalism called positive freedom, which split off because of the inadequacy of laissez-faire prescriptions for the problems of complex industrial societies. It differs on the amount of organicism stressed. These revisionist liberal theorists, represented by the political theorist T. H. Green and many others, imply a limited organicism in their belief that the state ought to intervene to stop the excesses of powerful individuals exercising their rights exploitatively. They feel that the community is comprised of individuals who have a collective interest, often termed the public interest or the common good, which is the embodiment of the collectivity. Thus, they feel that individuals are best served by a cordial and mutually supportive relationship with fellow citizens, which depends on limiting excessive individualism. In our era, it is characterized by advocates of extensive welfare-state policies like those found in the Netherlands or in parts of Scandinavia.

Problems with the Organic or Positive-Freedom Idea of Liberty

The organic or positive-freedom idea of genuine liberty as collective participation, rather than protection from others through individual rights, has its problems too. One reason is conceptual and takes us back to MacCallum's analysis of the linguistic nature of freedom. Just as MacCallum suggests that we do not really mean to speak of freedom in an exclusively negative framework, solely as freedom from restraints, we also do not mean to refer to it only as the right to do something, in this case as the right to collective fulfillment in society. It is on this side that those who stress positive freedom concentrate, to the exclusion of freedom that involves choice and the absence of limitations on choice. Those who look fondly on positive freedom are surely right to acknowledge that viewing freedom as an abstract right that we somehow possess in lonely individuality is not what anyone really means by freedom, but they go too far in the other direction and potentially swallow up freedom as choice in the "freedom to" participate in an organic society in which too often people have no choice.

There is also the problem of conceiving of a whole, in this case a political community, as being greater than the sum of its parts. People must interact politically and individual rights must be limited by the requirements of social proximity, but it is hard to imagine why a polity should exist for any other reason than to provide a better life for its individual members than they would have without it. The larger society is not something mystical, above and beyond each of us interacting with others. The society is not some greater public interest placed on so high a pedestal that it devalues individuals.

This is a dangerous tendency in any theory that does not guarantee some basic individual protections through limitations on collective actions that may deny room for individual rights. Advocates of organic freedom often fail to consider individuals as important, regardless of their reciprocity with others that can enhance but not define their value as human beings and citizens. In their stress on community interests they can go too far in destroying individual liberty.

Still, the organic theory of liberty does face squarely the social and political dimensions of liberty. It recognizes that the advocacy of isolated and egotistic personal liberty ignores the political dimension of the life of a citizen. It is quite right to point out that liberty that guarantees an extreme atomistic individualism leads not only to social chaos but to less real liberty to accomplish what one needs or enjoys, and is often a license for selfishness by elites. As a complete theory of liberty, it leaves much to be desired, but as a series of valid insights and a corrective to negative freedom, it is worthy of respect.

SOCIAL LIBERTY AND THE BALANCE OF RIGHTS

The final category in our typology reflects our view and that of those who see the defects of both negative and positive liberty. It perceives problems with too much negative liberty, but resists organic outlooks on liberty as well. We call this the position of social liberty, because it recognizes individual rights modified by an appreciation of collective demands. Thomas Hobbes, for example, in his *Leviathan*[18] predicted that absolute liberty would lead to a "war of all against all" in a "state of nature," where life would be "solitary, poor, nasty, brutish and short." He argued that the strong would exploit the weak in the ceaseless competition for security in a world of finite resources, and that no person was so strong that he could afford to turn his back or sleep without fear of having a coalition of weaker people attack him and wrest away his gains. On the other hand, Hobbes saw that some liberty was valuable. In the same work he cautioned that all citizens must have absolute dominion over their own lives and bodies. Nobody could kill or torture them, even in pursuit of the all-important public order that he prescribed as the antidote for too much freedom, because order existed for people and not vice versa. The authors of our U.S. Constitution went even further. They eventually provided for negative liberties in the Bill of Rights in order to preserve individual integrity, but wrote a constitution that distrusted popular wisdom and made it difficult for a majority of citizens to control the organs of government in order to translate individual liberties into policy supportive of public needs. As Madison and Hamilton indicated in the *Federalist Papers*, they were afraid of a tyranny of the majority that, in their view, would be a passionate and undisciplined lowest common denominator. In the same vein, John Stuart Mill pointed out that lack of negative liberty would allow those in power to become a permanent establishment that would stifle the human potential in all of us. For example, the alarming lack of competitiveness in many legislative elections around the world, including U. S. congressional elections, is a cause for concern in this regard.[19]

The Case for Social Liberty

We agree without reluctance that some liberty (even much liberty, as Mill would have it) is necessary for individual citizens. We do not see, however, why such a recognition must be extended to its absolute limits. We maintain that just as there are good reasons to have liberty, there are also good reasons why there must be some limitations on the rights of individuals, in order to advance the public interest. We are still individualists, but recognize the political dimensions of our individual lives and consequently, we appreciate the rights of the collectivity that limit individual freedom. Along with Mill, we argue that individuals may pursue any kind of private behavior as long as it stays truly private—as long as it does not affect others directly and negatively. The moment others are intimidated or otherwise negatively affected by behavior, it is public and subject to public regulation for the good of the collectivity. Thus, the actions of the nineteenth-century robber barons deserved public regulation, because their individual liberties intruded in a rude manner on the lives of others. The liberty of all individuals (equal members of a collectivity, not a metaphysical community) must be protected in practice as well as in principle, not just the liberty of a chosen few with social "clout."

We wish to use the political community as a force to intervene in political situations to protect the liberties of all by curbing the liberties of those who advance them at the expense of others. We look to the modern state to accomplish this task by default, because it is the only sector in society today that has enough force to stand up to a General Motors or other multinational. Ideally, it is the only institution that can act in the interests of everybody without favor, at least in principle.

There are many thinkers who favor the concept of social liberty. They range from Hobbes who favored sweeping intervention in the name of order, to Keynes who favored action to cure material poverty,[20] to modern feminists who demand continued attention to affirmative action, to civil rights advocates. The variety of rationales for political limitations on individualism in the name of public interest constitutes an exhaustive catalogue. Social liberals as diverse as Freud and Bentham agreed on the need for a balance of individual and collective rights, in spite of differences on what constitutes the public interest. Freud, for example, justified social intervention on the grounds that human nature needs opportunities for harmless displacement of aggressions, if civilization is to avoid permanent war.[21] Bentham justified it because he thought it would secure the greatest good (the absence of pain and the presence of pleasure) for the greatest number in society—the theory of utilitarianism.[22]

Defenders of a concept of social liberty today agree that it is the major rationale for the modern, limited welfare state and our federal government's reason for entry into industrial regulation, environmental protection, national defense, equal rights, job supply, and a host of other tasks. It is virtually universally accepted. It is often claimed, with some merit, that the reason for such interventionist devices as Amtrak (The National Railroad Passenger Corporation) or the Tennessee Valley Authority in the United States is not an American desire to embrace social liberty, but a laissez-faire culture's grudging recognition of the necessity to accept it and to act in the face of repeated failure of negative liberty.[23] Analytically, what unites theorists of social liberty is the rejection of the extreme claims of collective as well as individual rights and a common embrace of a balance of these claims in a concept of a public interest that will integrate them, as it simultaneously prevents the excesses of either.

The objective is a range of balance between claims of individuals and groups that restrains the excesses associated with allowing complete individual freedom in a political framework. It prohibits the powerful from consolidating their hegemony through exploitation and it actually gives more usable freedom and better personal options by providing a greater opportunity to develop resources and skills in a sound environment. Under such a doctrine, everybody is subject to restraint of antisocial or exploitative behavior, yet suffers little restraint in many sectors of life. This involves a gamble that the concept of an identifiable public interest in the form of specified restraints on individuals will not make the whole so important that it allows individuals to be discounted.

Problems with Social Liberty

The major problem with the attempt to balance individual liberty and collective decisions that place liberty in a social context is that the balance in principle does not necessarily assist us greatly when we have to make concrete decisions about liberty in specific situations. A good illustration of this dilemma came in a recent referendum on massage parlors in Madison, Wisconsin. Among those who argued on both sides of the question as to whether they should be allowed to operate were those who were decidedly in favor of the concept of social liberty. Some contended that massage parlors were an obvious area where there was so little public effect that individual negative liberties ought to be dominant, and massage parlors left free to operate as they wished. Others insisted that what was at stake was the very quality of a society, the context in which people grow up and live; that to permit massage parlors was to reify negative liberty without any real interest in the broader social context. Similar debates swirl around the uses of nuclear power for generating electricity or the regulation of pornography in many major cities through zoning.

Dilemmas such as this one bother some people inordinately, because they believe that there is, somehow, a magic formula that we can invoke to decide what liberty really is or what commitment to liberty would really dictate in this or that specific situation. Alas, this hope is an illusion. There is no such formula. What we can do is understand several images of liberty, the conceptual and normative arguments for and against each; we can propose and argue for the best possible image of liberty, as we have. In every concrete decision, however, there will be no substitute for an ongoing process of discussion and argument about what liberty is and should be. This discussion can proceed far more easily when we have in mind how liberty is alternatively viewed, but in the end discussion and choice will have to go on—fortunately. It is what makes liberal democratic societies such a challenge to live in.

CONCLUSION

In the final analysis, none of these types of liberty has an absolute monopoly on truth. The laissez-faire position, advanced in order to protect citizens from arbitrary and ruthless treatment by the state or powerful private interests, is a valid one when such threats do occur, as they have throughout human history. Tyranny from whatever source is an ever-present danger and must be dealt with, if overall human political interests are to be preserved. Opening up gates, however, in the fence erected against public power, to allow the state to protect against private power misuse, often opens up a big gap that cannot easily be closed again. The state has an interest of its own and its power cannot be invoked from the heavens and then sent back at will. The gates are not easily closed and advocates of strong positive freedom must be very cautious that the public power they sanction can be controlled. Also, organic freedom does not remove the dangers of tyrannies of the majority, about which Mill and de Tocqueville warned. Something must be done to control them, if we are not to suffer the stifling conformity and loss of individuality that can gnaw away at the vitality of any political community. As Sir Isaiah Berlin writes,

> What is true of the confusion of the two [negative and positive] freedoms, . . . holds in even greater measure of the stretching of the word to include an amalgam of other desirable things—equality, justice . . . and the other ends that men seek for their own sakes. This confusion is not merely a theoretical error. Those who are obsessed by the truth that negative freedom is worth little without sufficient conditions fot its active exercise . . . are liable to forget that without it human life, both social and individual, withers away.[24]

We are left with the need for a reasonable balance between too much and too little individual freedom. We need to balance individual and collective interests by a theory of liberty that is moderate, one that succeeds in balancing freedom in principle with equal political access to it. The desirability of liberty as a reasoned value calls for restraint and points to some variation of the social liberal position as desirable. The great advantage of the social liberals is that they are cognizant that liberty should not be perceived in a vacuum: It is a social value with political implications beyond strict individualism.

NOTES

1. B. F. Skinner, *Beyond Freedom and Dignity* (New York: Knopf, 1971).

2. Isaiah Berlin has an excellent discussion of these issues and some of their claims and counterclaims in the introduction of his *Four Essays on Liberty* (London: Oxford University Press, 1969).

3. Ibid.

4. Alan Wertheimer, "Is Social Freedom An Empirical or Normative Concept?" Paper presented at Meetings of Midwest Political Science Association, 1974, p. 17.

5. For a good survey of Thoreau's writings, see Milton Meltzer, Ed., *Thoreau: People, Principles and Politics* (New York: Hill and Wang, 1963).

6. See Marshall Cohen, Ed., *The Philosophy of John Stuart Mill* (New York: Modern Library, 1961); Alexis de Tocqueville, *Democracy in America* (New York: Schocken Books, 1961).

7. Leonard Hobhouse in David Sidorsky, Ed., *The Liberal Tradition in European Thought* (New York: Capricorn, 1971), p. 99.

8. A good explanation and critique of this position is found in John M. Keynes, *The End of Laissez Faire*, in Sidorsky, *The Liberal Tradition*.

9. John Locke, "Second Treatise on Government," in *The Social Contract*, ed. Barker (New York: Oxford University Press, 1962).

10. He writes a column for *Newsweek* Magazine.

11. See Barker's introduction to his *Social Contract*, for an excellent analysis of the idea of social-contract theory.

12. The wisdom of these procedures notwithstanding, there are grave problems of implementing them universally, as the recent U.S. Supreme Court decisions in the Miranda case and others have shown.

13. Lon Fuller, *The Morality of Law* (New Haven: Yale University Press, 1964).

14. Gerald MacCallum, "Negative and Positive Freedom," *Philosophical Review* 76 (1967): 312-34.

15. See, for example, Plato, *The Republic*, Ed. A. Bloom (New York: Basic Books, 1968).

16. A good brief discussion of Hegel and Marx as organicists can be found in B. J. Diggs, *The State, Justice and the Common Good* (Glenwood, Ill.: Scott, Foresman, 1974), pp. 151-58. See Jean Jacques Rousseau, "The Social Contract" in Barker, *The Social Contract*.

17. Diggs, *The State*, p. 152.

18. Thomas Hobbes, *Leviathan* (New York: Collier, 1962).

19. See Albert D. Cover, and David R. Mayhew, "Congressional Dynamics and The Decline of Competitive Congressional Elections," in *Congress Reconsidered*, 2nd ed., ed., Lawrence D. Dodd and Bruce I. Oppenheimer (Washington, D.C.: Congressional Quarterly Press, 1981).

20. Keynes, in Sidorsky, *The Liberal Tradition*, p. 292.

21. Sigmund Freud, *Civilization and its Discontents* (New York: Norton, 1962).

22. Jeremy Bentham, *Principles of Morality, Utility and Legislation*, privately printed in 1780 in London and republished in many places.

23. For a good discussion of the pros and cons of the welfare state in the United States, see Dolbeare and Edelman, *American Politics*, 4th ed. (Lexington, Mass: D. C. Heath, 1981), especially Chapter 8.

24. Berlin, *Essays*, pp. lviii-lix.

SUGGESTIONS FOR SUPPLEMENTARY READING

General

Flathman, Richard E. *Concepts in Social and Political Philosophy.* New York: Macmillan, 1973.

Nelson, John S., Ed. *What Should Political Theory Be Now?* Albany: State University of New York Press, 1982.

Nisbet, Robert. *The Social Philosophers.* New York: Crowell, 1973.

Sigmund, Paul E. *Natural Law in Political Thought.* Cambridge, Mass.: Winthrop, 1971.

Liberty

Berlin, Isaiah. *Four Essays on Liberty.* London: Oxford University Press, 1969.

Fuller, Lon. *The Morality of Law.* New Haven: Yale University Press, 1964.

MacCallum, G. "Negative and Positive Freedom." *Philosophical Review* 76 (1967): 312-34.

Mill, John Stuart. *On Liberty.* New York: Dutton, 1951.

Oppenheim, Felix. *Dimensions of Freedom.* New York: St. Martin's Press, 1971.

Rousseau, Jean Jacques. *The Discourses* (especially the second). New York: St. Martin's Press, 1964.

Sidorsky, David, Ed. *The Liberal Tradition in European Thought.* New York: Capricorn, 1970.

Skinner, B. F. *Beyond Freedom and Dignity.* New York: Knopf, 1971.

Spitz, David. *The Liberal Idea of Freedom.* Tucson, Ariz.: University of Arizona Press, 1964.

Wertheimer, Alan. "Is Social Freedom an Empirical or Normative Concept?" Paper presented at Meetings of Midwest Political Science Association, Chicago, 1974.

5

Liberty and Equality—II

As we turn to equality, let us view it in its relationship to liberty. Today, liberty faces a number of threats, new instruments in the age-old effort by its enemies to destroy its exercise. In addition, equality itself can be viewed as an unwitting impediment to liberty, at least in an operational fashion.

Looking at some of these impediments to liberty, thought control is by no means something remote; it is a reality that is entirely possible everywhere through the technological and mass-marketing features of modern civilization. In the United States, for example, the mass media hold enormous sway. Who can say with confidence that its powers do not raise serious questions indeed about human freedom? Or consider the potential for manipulation available to those in and out of government, with access to computerized data banks that hold vast amounts of information about the general public.

Much concern has also been raised about the possibilities contained in psychiatry or even psychosurgery for dealing destructively with and radically violating the freedom of those who do not conform. Thinkers such as Thomas Szasz believe that the greatest contemporary threat to liberty in the United States lies in the abusive attempts to solve mental problems by making people conform and sometimes, indeed, locking them in institutions if they do not. This is a practice that the Soviet Union has long followed with nonconformists.

Pervasive as these threats to liberty may be, however, there is another set of threats that many political theorists have often singled out as a major danger. That danger is equality. There is scant doubt that equality has been one of the great concerns of political philosophers for the past several centuries, sometimes in social life, sometimes in economic affairs, sometimes in politics, sometimes in all three. It has been an aspiration of thinkers as disparate as Jefferson, Martin Luther King, Jr., and the great European socialists, but it has been feared for centuries, too, as a threat to human freedom.

There has been no agreement about just exactly what equality means, much less what value it has. To grasp what equality is all about is our first challenge. Clearly, if no two people and no two things are equal in the sense of sameness (as no two people are equally smart or no two snowflakes are the same), equality as sameness is not a natural concept. Instead, equality as a meaningful human value is about the concept of equivalency, about X and Y being equivalent to each other without being precisely the same. In effect, it means that they are both worth the same, even if they are physically different. No two dancers are the same, but they can be equally good. No two boxers are the same, but they can be equally powerful punchers. Men and women are not the same, but they can be equally valuable workers. No two citizens are the same, but they can be equally important and possess equal rights within the polity.

The central assumption of egalitarians has always been that while people are different, they are equal in being human beings, in sharing a single unity that is more important than their variations. The central political problem and area of dispute among egalitarians has always been how much of life should be directed toward the fundamental fact and value of human equality. What they seek is rarely so much an artificial sameness as the reasonable functional equality implied in having equal worth and say in the rights, benefits, and responsibilities offered by the political organizations regulating society. In other words, what they seek is universal membership, rights, and obligations in our polities, because all have the same moral stake in them. For example, the Civil Rights Act of 1964 in the United States mandates that places of public accommodation, businesses, and institutions that represent themselves as serving the public must offer their services to all comers, regardless of race, religion, and other irrelevant differences. So does the long-proposed Equal Rights Amendment to the U. S. Constitution. The concept of equal treatment before the law, irrespective of social differences, is another example. Those who subscribe to the expression of equality contend that the rules and regulations of society should apply to everybody in society equally, because everybody is of equal moral significance. Thus, a rich, articulate, powerful, white, male, Anglo-Saxon Protestant, charged with a crime, should receive the same treatment in the courts as a poor, inarticulate, politically weak, black woman charged with the same crime. A third illustration of the richness of the concept of equality is the socialist argument that all people ought to have equal incomes and access to goods and services. Again, they claim that people may have varying skills and talents, but they are all equally people, all equally valuable, and therefore ought to have an equal income in order to maintain and develop their lives. The next section of this chapter will focus on some of these position of political philosophers on precisely how equal we are and how we ought to be treated in polities as a result of that equality.

THE CONSERVATIVE VIEW

For a long time conservatives have argued that equality is not a worthwhile value at all, not least because it is so flatly at odds with what they see as the natural realities of life. They point to the readily observable fact that individuals are not born equal in size, appearance, intelligence, talent, wit, and a host of other characteristics. Nor do people evolve during life toward greater natural equality. Conservatives suggest that people are so far from equality in all characteristics that only a foolish polity or social system does not accommodate to this reality.

Many thinkers in every era from Plato in classical Athens to the present have gone further and maintained that we should accord deference and heightened opportunity to those who are superior by birth or achievement, in order to achieve a stable and satisfactory political and social system. They argue that societies must be led by superior people if they are to gain excellence and not suffer from the stupidity that results when the superior yield to the warped, albeit well-meant, demands of the inferior. Thinkers like Plato and Burke had no urge to condemn those who were obviously inferior. On the contrary, they sought a political society that renounced any equality, in part because they wanted to protect those not endowed with greatness and to put their destinies in the hands of the wisest in society. The inferior were not to be punished or belittled but, instead, paternalistically guided for their own good.

Those who exalt the fact of inequality do not agree on what aspects of the human person are the crucial ones. Some build their case on inequalities of intelligence and insight (as Plato did), others on wealth or aristocratic lineage and education (Burke), religious piety (the Puritans), military skill, technical and scientific understanding (in the view of many American technocrats), gender, race, and so on down an endless list. Much depends on which human characteristics a thinker most admires, but all agree that in what they consider the most important features of human capability there are massive differences that no nation may safely or honestly ignore. There is also disagreement on how rulers should be chosen. How can the inferior recognize qualities of greatness in those they select to rule? Should there be automatic hereditary political succession processes or should each generation be examined for qualities of greatness? Orthodox monarchists and Plato would disagree here, as well. In a sense, these critics of equality are not only saying that inequality is a good thing but are also counseling accommodating inequalities as political facts that political thinkers must deal with in building ideal polities.

The conservative position that people are not equal in talent and therefore should not be treated equally in politics is not very convincing. No matter what indexes of comparison we settle on, to say that people are not equal is true enough. We do not, however, share the inference for political equality that many conservatives draw from that observation. It is a major logical jump to move from the fact of clear patterns of human differences to an argument that people should not be treated equally in politics or elsewhere in society. This is a normative decision that cannot be made by dwelling on the undeniable empirical conditions of humanity. It is a question of whether, however equal or unequal they are, as living people they should be considered equal in moral worth and thus possess an equal right to political participation or a decent socioeconomic existence. These are matters that call for hard normative argument, not citation of the realities of inequality. Moreover, the demands made on citizens even in a highly participatory (and, therefore, highly egalitarian) democracy do not require excellence—only the recognition of self-interest and the vision required to imagine the general consequences of actions for others. Surely the Swiss are not better people than the Saudis who live in a monarchy, for example. Citizens in a representative democracy only tell the leadership what they want and perceive. And no authority, human or not, superior or inferior, can determine what people need with anywhere near the accuracy of a system that allows people to speak for themselves. The sophisticated egalitarianism required by participatory politcs may well be acquired through experience and education by ordinary people, if they are given enough reason to try to do so. Thus, conservatives do not establish their case for elite rule based on talent.

There is also a moral case to be made for political equality, beyond the truth that we are all competent participants in the human race. People who live in a polity have an equal stake in the quality of its institutions, policies, and provisions for the general welfare. The village idiot and the president of a large corporation are both equal in their need for national defense or environmental protection. Political theorists like Paine, Rousseau, and Camus believed that people should have equal say in policy decisions and implementations. Paine felt that people should not suffer the indignities of colonial rule, partly because it denied colonials an equal stake in their lives. He exhorted his fellow Americans to rebel, claiming that they had responsibilities to overthrow an unjust polity and to institute one that would allow for equality and liberty.[1] Rousseau was probably the most radical egalitarian in Western thought. He made sweeping moral claims on behalf of participation, decision making, and the equal distribution of political power. He saw that men were so interdependent that it would be self-defeating folly to treat them differently. Camus agreed, and argued that people must regard themselves as a unity. Any injustice done to one individual, no matter how remote, is a direct attack on the integrity of the solidarity of all human beings. In order to resist the enemies of life, people must regard all as their brothers and sisters, for only a unified rebellion against what he termed absurdity could establish life as a meaningful value. Life is an equal possession and value of all.[2]

In short, critics of a conservative position on equality make two main points. First, we are all equally human, equal in our worth as people, and possess an equal stake in our political communities. Second, we are all intelligent enough to play a valid political role, and none are so superior in any relevant way as to entitle them to rule others without their revocable consent.

The conservative position must be rejected, because it does not substantiate its case for inherent human differences as a justified rationale for political inequality.

THE COLLECTIVE FOCUS: EQUALITY AS CITIZENSHIP

Some political theorists view the citizen from a perspective that leads them to a different and more positive assessment of the value of equality in a political community. They see the individual differences among citizens, but contend that the differential qualities of individuals are not politically significant. The most restrictive position held by those who favor equality focuses on the human need for order. Thomas Hobbes is the spokesman for political theorists who define political equality and restrict it to order. He argued that human beings are equal in obeying the dictates of their self-interest and in pursuing personal gain. Their desire to acquire and possess creates the necessity for order as a means of insuring security in an interdependent society. They are also equal because all possess enough reason to be able to enter into a social contract, to give up most of their liberties in return for an equal stake in the political order under a ruler who has the power to enforce the social contract. Therefore, since people are equal in their natural desires and have an equal stake in maintaining peace, equality means the protection of human life for all through political order. Hobbes's formulation is simple and sweeping: individuals cannot escape their stake in the polity and each must submit to the Leviathan (ruler), who shows no favoritism in keeping order. Each citizen who transgresses on another must be dealt with swiftly (short of capital punishment or torture) with the full force of the state power.

Locke and others had a different view of equality as order. In his desire to protect the property rights of individuals, Locke's social contract provided an equal right for all individuals to protect their property, and if a government was established, all property owners had an equal stake in securing their property privileges, but no automatic right to property. Augustine had yet another view. He felt that all human beings in earthly societies were depraved and sinful and that they must all submit to the stern power of a king who ruled by divine right as vice-regent of the Lord in protecting citizens from themselves. Equality was harsh, but it allowed men who were equally sinful to persevere in the "City of Man" while on their way to the "City of God," where such stern measures were not necessary, since all who were permitted to enter had been purged of their sinful natures.

Under this concept, to be treated equally is to receive like treatment with other individuals in the same circumstances. It does not convey the meaning of any particular quality of treatment. Thus, in evaluating this or any other theory of equality, we must not confuse the word "equal" with something necessarily virtuous. We must look at the quality of the equality.

Those who view equality as residing in political order are on the right track, but they have not traveled a sufficient distance on it. Theirs is a concept that is as yet too restricted. To be sure, order can be conceived of only as applicable to all, or it would not be orderly, but we must ask whether it is worth the price they are willing to pay for it and inquire about what other values this concept ignores. In the typical case, Hobbes is willing to sacrifice much liberty as well as the rights of ongoing political participation in order to secure what could become the equality of a prison. To be sure, he hoped that complete order under a sovereign would allow most people considerable choice, even considerable laissez-faire, in their daily lives. But his pessimistic view of human nature, seeing people as evil enough to destroy themselves in a war of all against all if they are not restrained, made him very cautious and led him to build authoritarian tendencies into his theory. This is unfortunately common. Those whose main emphasis is on order pessimistically misread human behavior, if we are to believe modern behavioral psychologists and anthropologists who say that human behavior is not so easily predictable and is capable of much greater variance than Hobbesians admit.

Human beings need more than order or equality of property rights to make the most of their potential in a polity. Order is only a means to goals like social justice, political legitimacy, balanced liberty and equality, and responsive political communities. We ought to be more interested in asking what kind of order we are looking for—what values it will secure and protect—rather than making unsupportable claims that equality ought to be concerned with peace at any price. We need peace, but if we are going to have to pay too much for it, we are gaining only a Pyrrhic victory. If we have to enslave ourselves to get to heaven or live in a prison to avoid death, we must wonder whether this kind of equality is worth the sacrifice.

SOCIAL AND ECONOMIC EQUALITY

The socialist tradition of equality, which grew to maturity in the nineteenth century and is vigorously alive today, presents quite a contrasting image of what equality is all about. According to it, the reality of common humanity requires that all people obtain very nearly equal fulfillment of their basic social and economic needs. For many socialists this requires state ownership of the means of production, and for all of them it requires, at the least, active governmental planning and a welfare state. They reason that political communities necessarily exist for the mutual satisfaction of human needs, and that it does not make sense to allow access to great resources to some and to deny the benefits to others. If property is not held in common or if it is distributed very unequally, some people garner more than their just share of the limited resources. They squander and waste the greater part of it, while exploiting others by "stealing" their labor for ridiculously low wages or property shares. The result is a minority group of superrich whose monopoly of resources leaves the majority in relative poverty without access to what they need to survive, let alone flourish.

Socialists are angered by this monopoly. They make a strong case for equal property rights for citizens and condemn property accumulations that go beyond reasonable needs. The only property that they feel should not be subject to common ownership (thus giving each an equal and just share under the auspices of the community) or regulation would be that needed for strictly personal use and that could not be used to exploit others.[3]

While the theory that equality should mean socioeconomic equality is attractive, it is flawed to the extent that it slips into too great evaluation of the material dimension of life. As we argue in the chapter on justice, concern for substantive equality in material goods is an important value, but there are many needs and aspirations in life other than the exclusively material one that motivates the majority of orthodox socialists. Nor should we slip into the view that property relations are the sole important aspect of existence, which somehow explain all things and by a kind of "invisible hand" process, analogous to that employed by classical economists, will ensure that all will go smoothly in human existence, once equal property rights or common ownership of the major means of production are established.

Many Marxists have a tendency to fall under these illusions, but Marx himself was more careful, particularly in his classic discussion in *The Critique of the Gotha Program*. There he made clear, as he had elsewhere, not only that human needs are various and complex but also that formal equality in regard to property is far less an ideal than "each according to his needs," a rather different notion, which we will explore in the next chapter.[4] Equal rights, in short, encompass a great deal more.

EQUALITY AS SELF-GOVERNMENT

As we have seen, one important strand of Western political thought has been democratic equality, the equality of people as citizen-governors. Since democratic theory has played such a large role in our history of ideas and political practices, this sweeping special view of equality deserves a closer look.

Western democrats feel it is best understood as the equal power of all citizens to be their own sovereign rulers. Theorists like Locke, Mill, Rousseau, and Jefferson claim that the rights of self-government for all people constitute an adequate definition of equality, because governments make or influence virtually all of the significant public decisions in a society, including economic ones, and that equal decision-making status gives citizens all the power they need to enjoy a good public life. As we discussed earlier, democracy is a complex topic, and we will not review its many aspects again. In this context, we are examining the thesis that democracy secures all the equality needed in a political community.

Champions of the familiar Western concept of majority rule hold that true equality resides in allowing a majority to rule by enforcing its preferences (limited by individual rights to political dissent) on all who live in a polity.

Equality is served in this variety of democratic theory by creating the conditions for each person to fully exercise civil liberties and political participation, thereby having equal influence in policy decisions with all others. No one should be allowed any more than an equal share of influence or voice, because no one is better than anyone else or has the right to determine what others need. All are morally worthy. The only criterion for full enfranchisement is to be "a two-legged being who walks upright and does not have feathers," to paraphrase Aristotle's semifacetious image of a human being.

In pursuit of this, representative democrats maintain that popularly elected legislatures are the best mechanisms to represent majority views. To them, representation is not the same as determining what others need. It is merely an efficient system of consulting and implementing felt majoritarian needs. Thus, it insures sufficient political equality to merit enthusiastic endorsement. Locke and Mill assert that citizens get the equality they deserve through participation in open political procedures that allow access to representatives, fair play, and the right to try to become part of a majority in public opinion represented by public policy.

Representative democrats are essentially correct about political equality. Their claims are limited, however, because they afford genuine equality only to those who are on the winning side. If one happens to be on the defeated side—especially consistently—the equal opportunity to vote for representatives or policies is hollow, even if people have an equal theoretical chance to become part of a majority, with effort. Consistent losers may have this chance in situations where there is an almost equal split between partisans and where the swaying of a few minds could change the outcome, or in situations where there is no automatic favoritism or negative prejudice shown to proponents of a cause, regardless of its merits. The existence of genuinely pluralistic political communities that produce this kind of political equality is a rare phenomenon, though a noble goal. Virtually every polity has within its ranks groups of consistent losers in policy matters. Pervasive political equality requires an equal ability to mobilize majorities, and that is a deficiency in most political systems, including representative democracies that espouse majoritarianism.

This concept of equality also does not deal adequately with tyranny of the majority, the powerful and oppressive force of public opinion, and the intolerance of differences that forces itself on minorities. It afflicts even those who have the resources to try to convert others to their cause, but who cannot get a fair hearing because their appeal falls on deaf ears. Sometimes these minorities are "cranks," but in all too many instances they are people who have a heightened moral sense and the courage to speak out against the injustices that most people would rather not be reminded about. The conscientious resisters to the U. S. war policies in Vietnam, who spoke out throughout the 1960s, are a poignant example. These minorities were not served equally by a theoretically open representative system. Another important objection in the U. S political system is that making one's voice heard, lobbying, or seriously running for political office takes substantial sums of money. Being free to campaign does not guarantee equal access to the not-so-free marketplace of ideas in an era when presidential campaigns run over $100 million and congressional races are commonly passing the quarter-of-a-million point per candidate.

Some participatory democrats have suggested that the egalitarian defects of representative democracy will be overcome when universal and direct participation actually takes place.[5] They feel that participation will negate the effects of elite tyranny over the populace, whether it originates by design or accident. They reason that if all people govern directly, the problems of majority tyranny and consistent losers will disappear at the hands of a spirit of community.

Rousseau doubted this, however. Through his concept of a general will, which will not allow a community to act unless all share a single voice on an issue, he realized that equality as universal access to political participation by itself will not cure the problems of majoritarianism by an invisible-hand theory of community. Community and a "general will" must be sought and nurtured. They will not appear magically as a constant companion of participatory democracy. The hopes of the 1960s radical democrats and some modern technocrats, who see a solution to the egalitarian problems of democracy by merely bringing on line modern interactive communicative technology, do not consider such subtleties. Direct citizen participation, even if achievable by technology, would still be only procedural improvement over representative participation and would not deal adequately with tyranny of the majority. While majority tyranny is preferable to minority tyranny from the standpoint of the number of those oppressed, the usual participatory system is still subject to the problems associated with most democratic theories in regard to political equality.

Problems cannot be defined out of existence with vague references to community and no machinery to implement them. Consensus may be impractical, but it is an attempt to substitute something for majoritarianism. A solution of the problems of representative democratic theories based on limited participation rights does not eliminate the reality that there are winners and losers on any policy question where consensus is absent. Participatory democracy is valuable, because it allows losers to speak for themselves instead of through imperfect representatives, increasing access to potential majority formation—but it cannot make an unpopular minority more palatable to a majority conditioned to it. It is an improvement, but not fully satisfactory. Consensus is remedial, but it pays the heavy price of deadlock and inaction in the face of pressing problems, or else it must allow the opposition the right to refuse to obey the law or policy in question. This raises the disturbing possibility of the erosion of community-mindedness.

For these reasons—and also because the theory does not fully extricate itself from charges that universal rights of participation could not be effective, due to differences in articulateness, education, and social class, as well as the unpopularity of affiliation—we must reject participatory democracy as the full measure of a definition of political equality. Yet it is appealing for other reasons, as we detailed earlier. Thus, it is a commendable political theory and a valuable component of equality. Its pervasive rights of access to political decision processes make it broader than order, property rights, or any other theory of political equality we have examined, but it, too, does not go quite far enough.

A LAST POSITION

In the final analysis, in order to make the most of equality, we require a general doctrine of equality understood as basic human fairness in the context of public relationships. Indeed, all of what we have examined so far can come under a general doctrine of what many political theorists refer to as fairness, being fair to all persons by treating them equally in ways that they and their circumstances warrant. The philosopher John Rawls has recently argued this most cogently.[6] Implicit in such a doctrine is a carefully defined value of life that respects all human beings and assumes that each deserves to be treated with equal dignity.

Many thinkers agree that equality as fairness cannot embrace rigid formulas that treat all exactly the same way, because people's needs and circumstances differ radically. An example is the progressive income tax laws found in most industrialized nations, which maintain that the rich can afford to pay a higher percentage of their income in taxes and still live more comfortably than the poor, who would be left at the brink of starvation if forced to pay high tax rates. A 5 percent sales tax on food has a much more negative impact to a person on a minimum wage than a 5 percent tax on a luxury automobile to a millionaire; the same tax does not have a fair or equal effect on both. Thus, fairness dictates that the functional equivalent of equal treatment may not be literally equal. Nevertheless, it should be applied to people in different circumstances in a polity in such a way that each would receive an equal amount of what is really required: fairness and respect for human dignity, and provision for legitimate needs.

This theory is attractive. It focuses on a broad class of needs and situations that could conceivably encompass most of the problems needing equalization in a complex modern political community, from rights of sexual preference to guarantees of equal access to places of public accommodation. It is also congruent with satisfactory amounts of democracy. It does not restrict itself to rigid formulas that limit its practical effectiveness or moral content. Its major flaw is that it is so vague that it can be defined in virtually any way without stretching it out of proportion. It is so elastic when applied to equality that it has no obviously discernible form.

Thus, in order to embrace the strengths of equality as fairness, while avoiding its vagueness, our task is to tighten it and focus it on the specific problems of political communities. The specifics of a good equality theory ought to change as they are applied to different societies, but the valid moral principles behind specific prescriptions remain, regardless of given applications. A reformulation of fairness as the need for a public policy of treating obvious equals equally, and unequals unequally, within a framework of equal opportunity for all, will accomplish our goal. As we have seen, people are generally the same in their politically relevant characteristics and each citizen's claim to participation. They have the same political stake in a polity that consists of moral equals interacting with each other through common democratic institutions and culture. Thus, all citizens ought to have an equal political input into their political system, ought to expect equal enforcement of the laws, and should receive equal justice in the courts. As we shall argue in the chapter on justice, people are also equal, if not the same, in their basic economic needs, and their society ought to guarantee them the realization of their equality.

In many other areas of life, however, people are scarcely equal. They are not equally good students, adept baseball players, skilled medical doctors, or competent mechanics. Here the essence of fairness, and thus equality, is to treat them as unequal and allow those who are especially talented to pursue the right to be superior, to be unequal, even to get more rewards, within some limits. But we argue that this is fair only when people who are unequal in various characteristics start out with equal opportunity. Society should provide for an equalizing factor that puts all people on a starting block that has the same length of track in front of it, recalling our analogy to a footrace run on an oval track. Thus, people who are victims of racial, religious, sexual, or any other discrimination should be given increased training and/or privileges of access to economic, political, or other kinds of opportunities (the equalizing of the track) in order to erase past inequalities—to equalize the running distance, so to speak. Equal rights are not just clichés. They must be the heart of enforceable, fair, public policies.

This norm of equalization of opportunity takes on characteristic prescriptive forms in contemporary Western applications. It stresses economic opportunity through such devices as minority training and hiring programs (for example, those the American automobile industry adopted after the Detroit riots demonstrated the discrimination built into their personnel policies); affirmative action programs, which demand that employers and others seek minority persons and women in order to equalize personnel, students, or whatever is being counted; job-training programs, which give vocational training to the victims of inadequate schools; and equal right statutes and other devices that seek to reverse discrimination patterns of centuries.

Educational opportunity is another area of concern to an equalization-of-opportunity approach. People cannot succeed unless they have the quality preparation that allows the poorly prepared to "catch up" and have an equal chance at educational benefits, from jobs to social consciousness. Thus a broad range of institutions and programs are needed here, too. Similarly, political opportunities like voter-registration aid, equal apportionment, and civil-liberties protection helps those who have been effectively drummed out of the polity, by providing them with a citizen's rightful political efficacy.

These purposes may sound pleasant and worthwhile, but it would be a grievous mistake not to understand that they are, in fact, extremely difficult to achieve. The way is hazardous and by no means certain. The unpleasant truth is that many government programs to open up opportunity have not worked and the problems have often resulted from too much—more than too little—money. People cannot be easily trained, jobs are not always available, and attitudes die hard. Above all, efforts to achieve greater political and economic equality, as well as general opportunity, face the redoubtable force of those who are simply not interested in surrendering what they have in order to accomplish this objective.

In addition, great care must be taken to structure these programs so that they do not result in reverse discrimination, making children pay for the sins of their parents. This can be avoided, but it takes planning, great resources, and care. One way to achieve a fair piece of the pie for everybody, of course, is to sink enough resources into the project to prepare an expanding pie. Many people fear that equality as fairness and equality of opportunity will result in a kind of leveling down in society. The reality is, however, that part of the aspiration of equality as fairness is to allow obvious unequals to reach their proper level. People who have a really equal opportunity at something and who are at all superior will excel. Furthermore, such excellence will be the result of genuine merit, not the result of unfair competition that gives winners an unjust advantage and losers a legitimate complaint. Soundly conceived in such a broad manner, equality as fairness is freedom from prejudice, favoritism, or official fraud, a theory of equality that could ensure citizens the fairness that human beings in a polity deserve, which is the only valid justification of political communities.

This approach is the best that we can do in defining and applying the norm of political equality, because it covers a sufficient range of human concerns to blanket virtually all of life with a desirable application of the value. Therefore, we conclude that equality as defined here is an invaluable component of any political theory. It is necessary but not sufficient to allow a good life to flourish in a complex political community. While it is not the definitive answer to all of our problems, it is powerful enough to command our sympathetic consideration.

LIBERTY AND EQUALITY

Now that we have explored some theories of equality, we return to an earlier theme: the interrelationship of liberty and equality. Everybody desires some kind of freedom and each of us wants to be considered as good as anybody else, but we cannot have everything. These desirable values have an unfortunate tendency to conflict in their interactions within a polity. We simply cannot have a broad spectrum of liberties as well as simultaneous equality in everything. Our alternatives thus are limited—we have to make choices between values. The task at hand is not so much simply a matter of finding an artificial balance between them as it is the need to recognize that their interactions as values need to be reconciled and accommodated to each other.

For instance, we cannot have unlimited liberty of property rights and do much about providing equal opportunity for people in economic life. Nor can we provide people with a basically equal and decent environment without interfering with the freedom for both individuals and businesses to do what they wish with their property. Similarly, how can we exalt the rights of conscience to untouchable heights and yet expect that we can have a democracy of equal citizens, all subject to law? Nor can we doubt that the existence of a democracy that provides equal citizen participation may well lead to the passage of many laws that restrict individual liberty.

Instead of lamenting that equality and liberty will often be in conflict, we should consider what can be done about this unavoidable reality. There are only three basic alternatives. We could concentrate on liberty alone, on equality alone, or we could try to accommodate them to acquire the maximum advantages of each.

The option of sticking with liberty and abandoning equality is not a very fruitful one. Without guarantees of equal treatment and rights for people who do not have great natural abilities or favorable backgrounds, and without unlimited resources and a constantly expanding frontier available to all comers, the potential for violent or debilitating social conflict over resources and status is too great. Such conflict could not help but stifle human development, because it would siphon off too much effort of individuals and communities alike into mechanisms for competition and coping with its effects. It would leave precious little human energy or motivation that could be directed toward political accommodation and common betterment.

The greatest irony would be that in such a society liberty could hardly flourish. Even the most powerful and wealthiest might have little chance to enjoy their freedom, and it seems doubtful how much liberty the average citizen would have in a world of such great potential of real political and economic inequalities.

To be free is fine as long as freedom is adapted to the characteristics of the political communities that citizens need to reach their most desirable quality of individual existence. Unfortunately, liberty without equality will not supply that by itself. Efforts to ameliorate the problems of liberty alone are reflected successfully in theories of social freedom that go a long way toward supplying that kind of social framework, precisely because they are not pure theories of freedom. Instead, they incorporate the valuable restraints that equality can put on liberty.

Similarly, equality alone in any pure sense is not a morally accepted option, either. Sweeping and unlimited stress on equality would drastically limit freedom. An unrestricted requirement that people must have the same chances, rights, resources, skills, rewards, and status could prevent the flowering of any individual differences and talents. People are talented in different areas, and forcing them to practice the same skills would produce mediocrity in all pursuits. A law firm of physically gifted but mentally mediocre partners would be in just as bad shape as a professional basketball team with good scholars who cannot run, dribble, and shoot.

Liberty is too precious to abandon. Even though it is not an unmitigated blessing, we must carefully justify any interference with it, whether in the name of equality, justice, order, authority, or what have you.[7] By the same token, we must and can justify limits on equality, since in the theory of social liberty or equality of opportunity, limitations in the name of vague concepts of a public interest will not do in this regard, either. The need must be clear and present and the remedy appropriate and limited enough so that it will not destroy the need served by liberty. Human beings need to be free as well as equal, and liberty cannot be reduced too far, lest human development be lost sight of and the specter of regimented dehumanization arise. Equality alone can be just as pernicious a form of degradation as unrestricted liberty. We need to have ample amounts of it to modify the extremes of liberty and to guarantee that liberties are available to all, but any more than that can become a remedy worse than the disease.

Therefore, with the rejection of both pure liberty and equality as viable options, our alternative is some form of rough balance and coexistence between liberty and equality within a political community. An accommodation of these values is the only way to secure the maximum possible benefits of both. Their operation in concert has the desirable effect of blunting the liabilities of each one as a separate entity. Even though they do not affect each other in any direct mechanistic balance, they clearly do have a great effect on each other. Like vintage blended whiskies or pipe tobaccos, they can mellow each other and produce a smooth mixture of finer characteristics without the individual "bite" of each ingredient alone.

Such a blend of the two values can be accomplished in several kinds of political orders. It is not the exclusive province of democracies and has been achieved at times in virtually every type of polity. Democracies with strong citizen participation in decision making have the greatest likelihood, however, of reaching and maintaining such a state of affairs, because they tend to tap the natural pluralism (not merely pay lip service to a pluralism perverted by imperfect democratic institutions) of large, reasonably free populations that have guarantees of equal opportunity and that will keep monopolistic establishments from forming and stifling diversity.

It is important to note, however, that a blending must be secured with the political interests and needs of the citizens firmly in view. Any blending that is in the interests of a ruling class and merely co-opts citizens is fraudulent in conception as well as operation and will not accomplish what it ought.

We should not approach this concept simplistically. These values do not have to be in a state of perfect balance in order to fulfill their moral functions. Values are not pieces of gold in a jeweler's scale that is constant and merely detects differences of weight. Societies are constantly changing and so are their ideas of the best values. A realistic balance between liberty and equality must have both values present in significant quantities, but it can and sometimes should put more weight on the side of one or the other. A morally acceptable set of political values and prescriptions should be subjected to and the result of a lively political process resulting from the contributions of all citizens. It must adapt itself to the ever-changing needs of people that result from shifts in their environment, as past policies and institutions combine in a kaleidoscope of social interactions. As conditions change, there is a need for different values and political prescriptions to be emphasized. Yesterday's prescriptions may be obsolete tomorrow and the day after they may be valid once again, albeit in a different way. What is required above all else is the constant attention and perception of political theorists, policy makers and citizens, so that the many possible combinations of these values may be culled for the most appropriate one in any given political situation.

We think that the appropriate balance for the United States and the Western world in the emerging postindustrial era should have four aspects. First, we would continue to encourage the movement of recent years that has abolished more of the legal barriers to the free pursuit of individualism in such areas as dress, sexual behavior, philosophy, and living arrangements. Here is a realm of individual freedom that seems to us to be vital for the development and growth of each individual person, even those who choose to conform. This would include a steady maintenance of basic political liberty to make one's voice heard.

At the same time, we must face the fact that the Western world, indeed the entire world, faces an inexorable crisis brought on by our unending interest in economic development and the consequent pollution and destruction of the environment. As Robert Heilbroner points out in his grim book, *The Human Prospect*, this will involve not just a restriction of private economic liberty of business but also a limitation on individual desires for endless and expanding consumer freedom.[8] It also requires a continuing education about the ecological consequences of some of our more foolish consumer choices, so that we can restrain ourselves instead of having a distant center of power do it arbitrarily. Our concern for equality, not just an equally decent environment but indeed an equal survival, requires attention to this equality at the sacrifice of this dimension of liberty, the liberty that is literally threatening to kill us.

Third, in order to achieve the equality of opportunity to participate politically and to have a chance to succeed in what we seek to do in life, to have a chance to make choices, we will have to undertake action that will undoubtedly require further restrictions of excessive economic liberty and the liberty of property rights, subjects we discuss further in Chapter 7. We know the truth is that we cannot have pure liberty and equality together and in this case, as in others, it will be necessary to restrict property rights in order to maximize political equality and the liberty to develop for all people.

Neither pursuit of individual liberty wherever possible nor the restriction of liberty in the name of survival, opportunity, and equality through the use of the state will, however, ensure progress toward the highest aspiration we seek in the accommodation of liberty and equality, the furtherance of authentic individuals united in an awareness of common humanity. Our theory of authenticity holds that people need and ought to have arenas of both solidarity and spontaneity in social and political life. No institutions or programs or allegedly perfect balances of values can reach this point.[9]

We distinguish, from the first, simple equality from solidarity, for people can be equal in all respects before the law as well as before each other, and at the same time remain strangers. They can have no way to relate to one another across the barriers of mistrust bred from the impersonal nature of an electronic society that isolates each in a cocoon of relationships to institutions and aggregates, instead of familiar personalities. Clearly, this is an outcome we must avoid.

The particular relationship of equality and liberty prescribed by this kind of approach is a mixture of solidarity and individual freedom. If citizens are secure in the knowledge that their needs will be satisfied, with reasonable effort on their parts, through an economic and political equality that recognizes individual variation, and yet know that they will have great liberty for political, intellectual, and personal choice, then perhaps they will someday have much less to fear from others. There might not be the terrible compulsion toward conformity and majority tyranny that currently is an understandable defense mechanism adopted by people who half-consciously resist, being submerged in a whirlpool of lost identity through mass bureaucracy, while surrendering to the fear of being different. The provision of the necessary and equal security for authentic individualism in conjunction with equality that does not operate through remote institutions and employs considerable participation of citizens in political structures is the great objective of this process.

If diverse people can relate to "real" people and not to faceless statutes and regulations through countless bureaus full of recorded announcements and impersonal video display terminals, then they have less to fear by being individuals. Liberty would be back in style as long as it did not extend to the point of depriving others of their needed equality or human survival. Perhaps people, no longer fearing each other, might come to like, enjoy, and respect each other—and human solidarity might grow and use modern technology for liberating purposes. Equality and freedom could grow in a polity operating on a humanly proportioned plane, not one designed for the convenience of data-processing machines and adapters of mass-production efficiency to political situations.

A perfect balance between liberty and equality is obviously utopian, but it could never be a final panacea. It would be merely a temporary adaptation of some basic principles to a set of circumstances that will change. The forms it might take are impossible to suggest neatly, because the relations would be ever in flux and because this ideal has more to do with the spirit of human interaction than the laws and forms of government that might assist its realization. Moreover, as is true for all political theories, there are no guarantees that it would work as well as its proponents claim. Still, even if it is not a panacea, it is a suggestive theory of what the correct accommodations of liberty and equality ought to be in the postindustrial world as it approaches the twenty-first century.

CONCLUSION

The issues of liberty and equality thus converge in a theory that accommodates them through norms of considerable economic and political liberty, equal opportunity, and social liberty, taken together. Liberty and equality cannot stand alone, because there are no such things—only specific liberties and equalities in one or another area of life—and because they often conflict with each other. Nor can we look at equality and liberty in a framework that ignores other root political values such as democracy, justice, and political obligation. We cannot somehow escape the terrible complexities of trying to balance multiple values by harking back to such a simple world as the one Rousseau imagined as the beginning of the human experience. No doubt we would not want to do so, either, because that would mean abandoning the fruits of our development along with its liabilities. Instead, we agree with Rousseau that we must develop the functional equivalent of simple nobility by adapting it to the problems and demands of our age. We need to strike the right balance among our values to find a political community that allows individualism and community to flourish simultaneously. There is no other way for modern individuals that will allow the maximum possible human development and provide the fruits of meaningful private lives in a noncoercive, responsive public sphere. There is no other way to experience the politics of accommodation, if not respect, in a postindustrial era. There is no other way to avoid the grave risks of destructive conflict. In the final analysis, we have nothing more than our values and moral vision to fall back on. There is every evidence that these will serve us amply if we will only use them.

NOTES

1. Thomas Paine, *Common Sense* (Garden City, N.Y.: Doubleday, 1964).

2. Albert Camus, *The Rebel* (New York: Vintage Books, 1956).

3. See George Lichtheim, *The Origins of Socialism* (New York: Praeger, 1962).

4. Karl Marx, *The Critique of the Gotha Program*, many sources.

5. Pateman, Carole, *Participation and Democratic Theory* (Cambridge: Cambridge University Press, 1970).

6. John Rawls, "Justice as Fairness," in *Contemporary Political Theory*, ed. Anthony De Crespigny and Alan Wertheimer (New York: Atherton Press, 1970).

7. See Richard Flathman's remarks on this in his *Concepts in Social and Political Philosophy* (New York: Macmillan, 1973), p. 264.

8. Robert Heilbroner, *The Human Prospect* (New York: Norton, 1974).

9. See Michael Weinstein's chapter, "Socialism and Humanism" in *The Politics of Community*, ed. J. Orenstein and Louis Patsouras (Dubuque, Iowa: Kendall/Hunt, 1973). Marshall Berman, in his *The Politics of Authenticity* (New York: Atheneum, 1970), gave it a convenient name.

SUGGESTIONS FOR SUPPLEMENTARY READING

Burke, Edmund. *An Appeal from the New to the Old Whigs.* Indianapolis: Library of Liberal Arts, 1962.

Gans, Herbert. *More Equality.* New York: Pantheon, 1973.

Heilbroner, Robert. *The Human Prospect.* New York: Norton, 1974.

Hobbes, Thomas. *Leviathan.* Many publications.

Lewis, Michael. *The Culture of Inequality.* New York: New American Library, 1978.

Lichtheim, George. *The Origins of Socialism.* New York: Praeger, 1969.

Orenstein, Jeffrey, and Louis Patsouras, Eds. *The Politics of Community.* Dubuque, Iowa: Kendall/Hunt, 1973).

Plato. *The Republic.* Many publications.

Rousseau, Jean Jacques. *The Social Contract.* Many publications.

Sharp, Gene. *Social Power and Political Freedom.* Cambridge, Massachusetts: Porter Sargent, 1980.

6
Justice

People talk about justice and fairness almost as much as they talk about the weather. It is an everyday subject that seems to come up endlessly. We discuss justice in connection with jury decisions and prison sentences; we have opinions about the fairness of our pay—and of other people's pay; we comment on the fairness of professors' grades and Academy awards; we talk about the justness of government policies, friends' criticisms, and, above all, our own treatment in life. In the process we express our own (often unconscious) theories of justice, individual and social, political and economic, human and natural. We refer so frequently to justice or fairness because we all assume it is a good thing, exactly as we take for granted that injustice is a bad thing. We all favor a just society, justice in the courts, a fair salary; and we are quick to denounce what we take to be injustices, especially when we suffer them.

Of course, however, people disagree about what justice is, both in principle and in specific situations—and they always have. Day after day people dispute the justice of calls in sports, whether justice is served in one or another ordinary criminal case of drug dealing, or whether one family member or another has treated them justly. They argue as well over the justice of decisions by the Supreme Court on abortion, or public regulatory agencies' rate formulas for gas and electric companies (and consumers). We may even argue over justice with the policeman who hands us a speeding ticket or the Internal Revenue Service agent who challenges our tax returns. Justice is clearly a major issue in politics, deserving our attention, because it is so much a part of our lives and because we disagree about it so often.

This chapter examines the nature of justice. It delineates what the major alternative visions of justice are, and suggests a possible resolution to the continuing disputes over justice. This is no easy task. We use the words justice and fairness often enough, and we have our own intuitive understanding of their meanings in different contexts, but it is quite another thing to formulate and defend a clear notion of justice.

VIEWS OF JUSTICE

If we can say that there is a just law, a just welfare policy, a just war, or a just society, then justice covers a great deal of ground. Clearly it is a rich concept, capable of mulitple uses, with a variety of meanings and inferences. Yet the extraordinary richness of the concept should not lead us to confuse it with all moral judgments in or out of politics. Justice is by no means the only moral value. It is obviously different from other values, such as love or human sympathy or charity. Nor is justice the sole political value. Whatever justice is, it is not the same as liberty, obligation, or equality, although it may involve them and promote them. There are limits to justice, then, however broad its reach and frequent its sway.

Our central concern here is precisely what justice is. We cannot answer that query simply by pointing out the limits of its reach in morality and in politics. Instead, we need to explore the universe of ideas of justice, which encompasses four main versions.

First, we consider views that locate justice in natural or divine laws, rather than human ones. These views hold that such higher laws are the standard for justice and that just individuals attempt to adhere to them as perfectly as they can. Second, we explore the familiar perspective that justice exists in statute law or in a set of procedures that are intrinsic to law as we know it in the Anglo-American world. According to this idea, the just citizen is one who follows the law, and the just law or legal decision is one that accords every person due process of law. Third, we examine concepts of justice that derive from considerations of utility, of what is the greatest good for the greatest number. Jeremy Bentham, the nineteenth-century English philosopher, was only one of many thinkers who have argued that the just society is one that seeks the general public good as its primary goal, defining the just citizen as one who cares about the greatest good above all else. While some utilitarians virtually equate justice and the greatest happiness (utility) principle, others say that utility is not justice itself, but superior to it and a valuable replacement for it. In this context we also consider the work of the celebrated modern theorist of justice, John Rawls. Finally, we look at what we call the ordinary-language definitions of justice, those that see justice as what is rightfully due to people, including such ideas as merit, effort, equality, or need. These four require considerable discussion, because we use some or all of them whenever we speak of justice, and because in a combination of them probably lies the proper standard of justice.

Divine and Natural Justice

Perhaps the oldest view about justice is that it is found in laws that are natural or divine in origin, rather than man-made. An ancient example of a divine conception can be found in the Old Testament's Law of Moses, the Ten Commandments. According to the Hebrew Bible or Old Testament, faithful adherence to the commandments is God's will for mankind guarantees the just life. Two quite different and more contemporary illustrations of a divine standard of justice are to be found in pacifist Quakers' frequent civil disobedience to oppose the Vietnam War and in Martin Luther King, Jr.'s, systematic campaign of civil disobedience to promote civil rights for blacks. Both appealed to laws of transcendental justice. Like Moses before them, both argued that justice is not for men and women to determine, nor is it the province of human laws, unless they accurately reflect divine will. Justice is of God and His ways.

With less emphasis on divine justification, other thinkers have sometimes invoked nature and its laws as the appropriate criteria for justice. For example, Henry David Thoreau approved both nonviolent and violent acts in defiance of government. His argument was that nature was our proper ruler and its rules were more than enough for those who sought to live rightly and justly. Many nineteenth-century anarchists, especially the Russian Peter Kropotkin, claimed that government and its laws always violate the justice that can be achieved only under the guidance of the natural order. Finally, many of those who are most concerned with the environment, ecology, and the energy crisis repeatedly speak in terms that show that they believe we are transgressing implacable laws of a sovereign nature that we dare not ignore any longer.

The enduring emphasis in Christianity on divine laws, the interest in the environmental movement in natural laws, and the persistence in traditional Africa and modern Islam of divine regulations all remind us today that the appeal to natural or divine standards of justice is by no means a phenomenon of the past. Yet it is also true that most Western philosophers and many Americans do not seem to think or talk in these terms about justice very often anymore. This is due partly to a widespread, though hardly unanimous, decline of confidence, among intellectual elites in this age of skepticism, that there is a divine or natural standard of justice. The examples of King and of thousands of religious conscientious objectors to the Vietnam War teach us, however, of the other side, of the many for whom justice is not ours to define or determine. For them justice lies in the provinces of God or nature. So does the extensive activity of Christian conservatives in polities today, who insist they are followers of God's laws. There are still many who glance up to their heaven for the guide to justice.

Both the divine and the natural approaches are necessarily incomplete as versions of justice, unless they include a specific discussion of the substance of justice in each case. Mere stress on justification, whether divine or natural, does not get us very far without a corresponding consideration of the substantive principles that accompany a justification of justice. These vary widely in natural or divine justifications. For example, at times the Old Testament makes justice a matter of retribution, whereas the New Testament makes the heart of justice forgiveness. Yet both views have a notion of justice grounded in a divine criterion. The situation is no different among natural theories of justice. The nineteenth-century American W. G. Sumner argued that natural justice supports a highly competitive capitalist society where merit is the norm of justice. Thoreau, on the other hand, thought the message of nature was equality and need. Thoreau and Sumner agreed on the standard of nature, but disagreed on the substance of what nature teaches.

This problem with these traditional approaches to justice does not rule out theories that employ a divine or natural justification. Simply stating, however, that justice is divine or natural in origin tells us little about the content of justice, and it ignores the multitude of conflicting opinions regarding the content of justice, whether divine or natural. The case for justice must be demonstrated, not merely asserted.

In this context one must ask, How does one find these higher forms of justice? Intuition and faith clearly play a major role for many religious believers who find justice in their god's teachings. For some skeptics this is a hopeless approach that turns the subject of a serious moral issue over to emotions and subjectivity, though for believers there is nothing subjective whatsoever in their understanding of truth. Others who call on an absolute natural or divine standard see reason as the means that leads upward to truth. Reason, sometimes termed "right reason," they contend, can open the deepest secrets of the universe.

This was the view of Plato, who argued that long and demanding study was necessary before reason could penetrate to the highest truths. Other theorists have believed that right reason is available to all of us on a much more ordinary basis. This was the democratic conviction of Thomas Jefferson and Tom Paine, both of whom believed in natural rights and thought everyone could understand what they provided. In any case, confidence in right reason leads to the same problem; those who suggest it often disagree on the content of justice. Either right reason is very fallible or most people who have employed it have been deficient in reason, because so many differing interpretations of justice crowd the stage competing for the spotlight. Indeed, right reason has led men and women in so many directions that skeptics cannot help but express caution about the reality of right reason. This does not mean there is no right reason—or natural or divine law. Many of us believe they exist, but they need to be argued carefully and fully, and never simply announced as if they were an obvious fact.

Procedural Justice

Americans are familiar with another concept of justice: legalism or proceduralism—the idea that justice involves guaranteeing due process of law or, more broadly, following the law. We say a just court is one that follows the law in a trial; a jury renders a just verdict when it acknowledges the facts and adheres to the appropriate rules for deciding cases; a policeman gets a warrant before searching our home or else he is violating our legal rights to justice under the Constitution; citizens act unjustly when they break the law by cheating on their income tax returns.

Those who are sympathetic to procedural justice take for granted that justice involves adhering to law, because they assume law embodies a set of procedures that make it the best possible instrument for justice. Obedience to the law ensures justice as long as the law contains attributes that proponents regard as central to its very being. Laws that lack these features are not really legitimate laws. Lon Fuller terms these standards the "inner morality" of the law, an apt characterization of the belief that we obtain moral justice only within a procedurally fair legal system.

Proceduralists argue that the uniform and equal application of law to all citizens is the most important legal norm. To avoid unfair discrimination and arbitrariness is the highest objective of a lawmaker. It is no simple matter to decide when any law is arbitrary, but law must not discriminate between two people in two identical situations in an inexplicable or illogical manner. If drunks who are picked up on day one end up in jail, while those picked up on day two are immediately released, the law is capricious and, therefore, unjust. Proceduralists also object to any distinctions in the law based on favoritism through nepotism, friendship, political association, bribery, or financial gain. All violate justice.

Other aspects of the law that proceduralists often cite as vital to justice include some of the most renowned and treasured provisions of the law as we know it. They include the idea that law must be publicized, that it must be clear, that laws passed today cannot refer to past actions, that no one may judge themselves under the law, and that disputes should be resolved as quickly as possible for justice to be done. Proceduralists insist that it is obviously unjust to hold people to laws they know nothing about, or to laws that they cannot comprehend. These criteria are simply a matter of giving people a decent chance in life. The prohibition of laws that apply to past actions is similarly justified. After all, how reasonable is it to punish someone for what he did yesterday when it was perfectly legal? Provisions for a speedy trial and impartial rather than self-interested judgment work in the same direction. Both promote a fair chance for everybody. Long-delayed trials deny fairness, as witnesses forget or die and money is endlessly spent for lawyers. Dickens, in his novel *Bleak House*, tells the unforgettable story of the case of Jarndyce and Jarndyce, a case that never ended but ruined all concerned.

The proceduralist ethic is familiar to us, but it is hardly the only way we think of justice. It is a partial version, at best. We sometimes say that laws are unjust or trial verdicts unjust, even though they meet every standard for procedural justice. The error of those who make the inner rules of law the exclusive content of justice is a failure to include substantive as well as procedural elements in their definition of justice. Many proceduralists do not appreciate that all the "fair" procedures in the world can mask purposes implicit in laws that offend our common notions of what is just. No matter how procedurally fair, laws may contain values or be designed for substantive objectives that we would consider unjust. Laws may consistently downgrade merit or equality or need in their effects, or they may work out in a manner that ensures that some people will be consistent winners and others consistent losers in the social, economic, or political system, inevitably provoking the cry that the laws are unjust even when they are procedurally fair.

A second problem with exclusively procedural concepts of justice is that they often build on naive assumptions. For example, some proceduralists assume that people have equal chances or resources in the legal process, when they do not—and possibly never can have. After all, procedures are just only when people possess or have access to roughly equal skills in the legal process, skills that usually require considerable money, awareness, and self-confidence to obtain. A person who has enough money or education to obtain a good lawyer obviously is in a better position to get justice in the courts than the old, sick person living on Social Security, the poor migrant worker, or an uneducated black. Only in a society in which all people are well educated and reasonably affluent can genuine procedural justice exist. Our society, like others, is as yet very far from this ideal.

Some pure proceduralists are also naive in their hope that justice can exist apart from the ongoing conflicts that are the reality of politics. The fact is that legal norms are not, and can never be, outside politics. Inevitably, proceduralists' emphasis on defining justice in terms of law and its inner rules is not neutral. Indeed, it often involves a bias toward the existing political and socioeconomic order.

Such difficulties with the proceduralist view, however, should not lead us simply to discard it as a legitimate aspect of justice. Respect for law and the equal and fair application of its central rules is important to any just society. Exclusive focus on the idea is insufficient, because it fails to include other vital dimensions involved in justice.

Utilitarianism

For some, legal proceduralism is not broad enough to include all aspects of an adequate theory of justice. Another theory is that of utilitarianism, which holds that justice is the achievement of the greatest good (or pleasure) for the greatest number. The classic theorists of utilitarianism, Jeremy Bentham, John Stuart Mill, and Henry Sidgwick, defended variants of this perspective in eighteenth- and nineteenth-century Britain. Bentham is famous in the history of utilitarianism for his detailed and ultimately unsuccessful effort to construct a calculus for weighing relative pleasures and their intensities. John Stuart Mill's contribution was his attempt to rank some pleasures as superior over others, an attempt that really suggested that some people's behavior was superior to that of others. Sidgwick contributed what many think was the most sophisticated defense of the utilitarian view. All of these thinkers and others since, however, have returned to the idea that justice is ultimately what brings most people the greatest pleasure or happiness.

Ordinarily utilitarianism contends that each individual experiences pleasure and pain and tends to achieve as much happiness as possible by maximizing pleasure and limiting pain. It holds that the just polity undertakes to accomplish policies that expand pleasure and reduce pain for the largest possible number of citizens. Utilitarian justice reigns when the political order serves to accomplish this end—the greatest good—for most people and certainly for a majority. It follows that the just government concerns itself with the general population, unlike those who link justice to the natural or legal rights of every individual. We agree with them whenever we feel it is necessary for the common good to restrain one minority or another—for example, to deny the "right" of murderers to kill or corrupt government officials to steal. We also sympathize whenever we complain about the advantages wealthy Americans obtain through inequitable tax shelters and write-offs or any other time when we perceive special interests triumphing over the public interest.

Yet the utilitarian vision of justice is flawed, because we can also easily imagine situations where what might be useful for the bulk of society would offend individual justice. Utilitarianism enshrines the principles of majority rule to the point of opening the door to tyranny of the majority. Because it might well be just from a utilitarian point of view to close down a troublesome newspaper, to persecute a rebellious black minority, or imprison selfish millionaires, utilitarianism hardly guarantees justice for all. We remember that the Athenians killed Socrates, convinced that he threatened the general interest of classical Athens, but we intuitively know that this was an egregious injustice. The point is that all of us normally (and rightly) think of justice sometimes in terms of individual persons; utility permits a good many individual injustices, if they promote the general good. While we may want to agree with many utilitarians that their search for the greatest good for the greatest number is important, we should not automatically confuse it with the sum of justice.

There are other objections to a utilitarian analysis of justice. Utilitarians are more concerned with happiness than they are with strictly ethical issues, among which we classify justice. Nobody denies that happiness is valuable, but there is no particular reason to equate it with justice. A second argument stresses that utilitarianism is not much good as a criterion of justice, because it is impractical. Critics ask how we can measure such vague notions as happiness or pleasure and pain. If we cannot measure them effectively, we cannot discover what the greatest good for the greatest number is and we will not be able to pinpoint utilitarian justice.

The most celebrated essay on justice in our time, John Rawls's *A Theory of Justice*, attacks the utilitarian position because it seems quite able to sacrifice justice for individuals in its search for the common good. Rawls charges that utilitarianism could, for example, support a system of slavery, even though few if any of us would agree that slavery is just. Like those who look to human, natural, or divine laws for justice, Rawls insists that justice requires an independent standard of definition, one free from the utilitarians' tendency to subordinate justice to utility. Rawls's solution is his idea that justice refers to two such norms. He contends that it involves equal liberty for all, and equal distribution of goods, as long as equal liberty is not sacrificed and any inequalities exist for the benefit of all people, especially the poorest.

There is good reason for agreeing with Rawls that the utilitarian outline for justice is inadequate, but there is less basis for believing that Rawls has resolved the problem of justice in politics. He offers in equal freedom a definition that few of us would recognize as connected with justice. Freedom, equal or not, clearly is about something other than justice. It is used in different linguistic circumstances than justice is—the free man is not necessarily the just man, nor is a free society necessarily a just society—so that the question becomes why Rawls and others propose to merge freedom and justice. Part of the explanation lies in the tendency of numerous thinkers to associate justice with any or all values they especially honor, since justice from Plato's time onward has often been considered the supreme value in politics. Another reason lies in Rawls's qualification that he seeks equal freedom. Equality in freedom or anything else is commonly associated with justice and, as we will see shortly, it is a serious view of justice on its own. But it is one thing to suggest that adequate freedom in a society requires that all citizens must have an equal amount of liberty and quite another to assert that equal freedom is justice. (For an extensive analysis of this point, see Chapters 4 and 5 on liberty and equality.)

Rawls's second criterion of justice is his principle of distribution. It is more familiar as an ordinary understanding of justice insofar as it stresses that goods should be distributed equally, but Rawls's modification of the norm to allow great inequalities in order to benefit the general population is really a covert form of the utilitarian justice he so vigorously attacks. Rawls's motivation for permitting inequalities is his belief that they can rebound to the greatest good for each person. Rawls believes that strict economic equality will prevent capital formation and thus interfere with normal economic development against the wishes and the self-interest of most people in any society. He may be right, but this calculation has little to do with justice and a good deal more to do with possible practical necessities of economic development. Rawls and the utilitarians would like the comfortable feeling that justice is useful and practical, but there is no necessary connection between what is right and what is practical.

Rendering Each His Due

Sometimes we do think about justice in procedural and legal terms and sometimes in utilitarian ones, but ordinarily we conceive of justice in another way that links justice with what is due to us. When we say we have gotten just treatment, we mean we believe that we have received what is properly ours, while we feel dealt with unjustly when we do not obtain "what is coming to us."

This common idea of justice makes a good deal of sense. It is built on a model of a world in which people are held to have justified claims and in which justice constitutes respect for those claims. The foundation of this belief is a conviction that every person deserves to be considered a special being who must be accorded respect and decent treatment. The implicit assumption is that people should be seen as ends in themselves, rather than as mere means to be used and abused as others may see fit.

The difficulty is, however, that few if any conflicts over justice can be resolved by declaring that we should respect people's claims about what is due to them. The reason is obvious. People disagree about what is due to them and to others. For instance, would giving each his or her due imply treating everyone equally, as a judge does who sentences every murderer to the same prison term? Some would say it must involve taking into account the circumstances of each murder—and each murderer. One murder was planned for years, another was done in a moment of passion. One murderer has a large family he is supporting, the other does not. Others would argue that the sentence should turn on the merit of the two murderers' previous lives. Murderer A led a decent, contributing existence until the murder, while B was a longtime criminal. Should they get the same sentence? Or consider the case where A gets a higher salary than B, merely because A works harder. Is that just? Yet, would it be just if B got a higher salary when he did better work, if the reason was that B was born smarter? Would it be just if A had greater need? Would it be fairer if they both got equal salaries, regardless of work, merit, or need?

Clearly what is owed to us as people is not self-evident. We must probe each of the several classic positions before we can weave a solution that will direct us to a satisfactory explanation of the elusive concept of justice.

What Is Due To Us Determined by Merit

A frequent test for defining justice as what is due to us is merit or desert. The idea is that we receive justice when we are rewarded according to what we are or do in life, as opposed to what we need or to simple equality. Surely, this view suggests, the productive worker deserves more salary than a hardworking but incompetent fellow employee. Similarly, it contends that the decent, law-abiding citizen deserves more respect than the criminal.

There are actually two forms of this argument, although in practice they are often mixed together or confused. One version contends that merit should depend on one's *personal qualities* rather than achievements—on one's intelligence or character or moral virtue. It holds that a just society would honor these characteristics—the human being's best features—and thereby demonstrate great respect for humanity. The other version concentrates on what people *achieve*, believing that contribution or productivity in life is a better basis for justice than any traits or talents one happens to have.

If we were to ask, for instance, what the desert test would define as a just economic distribution, the answer would depend on how we define desert. If we were to apply the test that stresses personal qualities, some qualities would particularly appeal to us as a proper basis for reward. Rewarding the hardworking is a good example. It seems somehow just to many people to take into account in paying people how hard they work (just as it often does to students regarding grades). Other qualities are less popular, however. Few of us would assign pay on the basis of raw intelligence or moral virtue defined in one way or another, regardless of work done or tasks accomplished.

On the other hand, if we apply a productivity test, justice involves rewarding those who are most successful in their jobs or in any activity. This is the justice principle of most economic systems, even to some extent Communist ones, though it is often modified for one reason or another in practice. It is, of course, the usual standard for awarding grades in colleges (the best paper gets the A), in deciding which athletes deserve the greatest respect (and, often, pay), and in deciding which politicians deserve reelection (they "produced"). There is no doubt, in short, that this criterion of justice is common to our way of thinking about the subject. Each of us employs it every day.

Neither of these two merit formulas is really satisfactory as a sole ground for justice in society, no matter how often we may think either is an appropriate standard. What we are or achieve depends to a large extent on chance, heredity, personal background, and general social conditions. This is so true that it is scarcely fair to give people vastly differential rewards exclusively on the basis of merit. Why should it be just to reward some people with money, status, or power disproportionately to others in similar situations, merely because they were born brighter than others or had access to better education, or because they are more productive at work as a result of being born more talented or having had access to superior training? The same point may be made another way by noting that advocates of the merit principle of justice sometime assume that everyone has an equal opportunity and it is therefore only just that those who succeed should do so. The truth is that powerful hereditary and environmental factors block the possibility of equal chances and call into question merit justice.

How far should we carry this skepticism of the role of our choices in structuring where we end up in life? It suggests a framework of determinism in life. After all, people do sometimes overcome—as we say—their upbringing or surmount some amazing hereditary handicaps. It also overlooks the fact that it usually takes a good deal of effort to realize innate abilities. It is not self-evident that all variations in what people accomplish are simply a matter of their environmental and hereditary background for which they deserve no credit. We cannot deny that there is often some "justice" to people's success or failure; the problem is that it is almost impossible to determine what proportion of anyone's achievement is due to his or her own choices and efforts.

While it may well be impossible to establish how much of our success we "deserve," it is clear that the view that we should be rewarded for our work is a third type of the merit theory of justice. If we decide that it is just to reward people only on the basis of the work they put in, regardless of what is produced in the end, we still cannot avoid the factor of environment. The efforts we make in our jobs, or whatever we do, are not exclusively our independent doing. Our socialization, our family, our upbringing, and our general social surroundings have a great deal to do with our attitudes toward work. Nor can we easily find a practical means to uncover what in our efforts is due to our choices and what comes from our background.

A second problem concerns the corollary of a merit test for justice: equal opportunity. In the real world opportunity can never be strictly equal, but if merit is to mean anything at all as a standard for reward, the competitors must have had something at least faintly resembling equal opportunity. A candidate who can control the electoral process through money and influence with the media obviously has a much greater chance for victory than a candidate who cannot; if the first candidate wins, it does not make sense to say he or she had an equal opportunity compared to his opponents and thus deserved to win; there was a much greater opportunity than that; similarly, it does not really make sense to say that a poor person who gets a bad education and is frequently sick from inadequate nutrition has an opportunity in the marketplace equal to that of someone who is born with a silver spoon in the mouth; it will be no surprise that the latter person will earn much more money in life, but who could convincingly say he or she deserved to?

The truth is that an embarrassingly large number of merit theorists defend a merit system, especially regarding incomes, without paying any attention to the question of equal opportunity. This is not acceptable. There are others, however, who know that anyone defending a merit system of justice must pay some attention to the question of equal opportunity. What is required at a minimum is an endeavor to increase equal opportunity in any society. This demands some effort to make sure that all people have the minimal necessities of life, and a decent educational system, so that the less advantaged can fairly join the competition that a merit view of justice defends. Some would go further and argue that state prohibition of a large (or perhaps any) inheritance is always required, to make sure that the children of the affluent do not succeed because of their inherited resources, rather than through their own achievements.

It is not clear where one should draw the line in the effort to increase equal opportunity. At some point, if efforts are unstinting, the state will be so involved in regulating people's lives and interfering with differences that there will be no room left for the differences that merit encourages and believes are just. Nonetheless, there must be concern with equal opportunity in every merit system of justice. Theories of justice that lack such concern are not serious; they are merely rationales for inherited advantage.

A third kind of doubt about the merit view directs our attention to its implications, if it is carried out to its logical conclusion. A thorough merit model of justice challenges both democratic political equality and equality before the law. Merit invoked in politics might mean that only the best minds or the most productive economic entrepreneurs should rule. Traditional democratic theory holds that regardless of merit every person should have an equal political voice. It might also mean that the "virtuous"—or the most economically valuable citizens—should get favored treatment in the courts. Proceduralist legal justice, however, maintains that equal protection of the laws should exist for all people, good and bad, productive or unproductive, hardworking or lazy. Advocates of a merit theory of justice, of course, rarely plan to apply it to either the political or legal realms, but it is worth noting how elitist the theory is. And we cannot avoid wondering why one aspect of life should be governed by merit and another by equality.

We make a fourth argument about the merit test by observing the curious fact that underneath its praise of talent or accomplishment is an implicit set of standards for what constitutes "good" abilities or "genuine" achievement. Proponents of merit certainly do not think it is just for society to reward either people who have unusual ability at fleecing the poor or the "hit men" of organized crime. In other words, not every achievement merits admiration or reward. Usually an implicit utilitarian or "public good" standard is present, acting to distinguish good and bad talent or accomplishment. Insofar as this is the case, the question becomes whether or not the merit test is a suppressed form of the utilitarian theory of justice and, therefore, vulnerable to the objections we raised about that view.

Proponents of the merit test insist that critics fail to understand two points. The first is that judgments based on merit are an inevitable feature of existence. Social differentiation will not go away. Second, they believe society needs to reward people of unusual capacities and productiveness. If it does not, rapid decline will occur. Both are important, practical contentions, but they do not establish a case for a merit theory of justice. After all, justice is a moral concept. It is about what ought to be. The fact that it may run head on into pragmatic realities does not necessitate a definition of justice that will perfectly accommodate them. What ought to be and what is or what is pragmatic are often in conflict. There is no particular harm in that. One may choose to have economic inequality for the practical reason that it may provide incentives for greater production of goods. Yet this choice does not so much require us to agree that justice is based on merit as it reminds us of the significant truth that justice is one value among many and not necessarily the value a society will, or should, rank highest.

In the end, the greatest puzzle about a merit conception of justice lies in the question of whether or not there is an appropriate distinction between what a person is or does as an individual—and therefore deserves—and the person as a member of the human race. Is the idea of justice, which is about what is owed to a person, to be grounded in the person as person, regardless of all else, or is it to be based on what the person as an individual has achieved as compared with other individuals? This is the great issue between the merit theory of justice and its classic opponent, the equalitarian position, which we examine next.

We should note beforehand, however, that many merit theories of justice are careful to construct a quite sophisticated system in which they insist on merit qualifications for justice in some cases and equalitarian qualifications for others. Following Aristotle's classical argument, they state that equals should be treated equally and unequals unequally. This means that where people are fundamentally the same, for instance as citizens, they receive justice only when they get equal consideration. For example, they all deserve equal protection of the laws and all should have an equal right to vote and to participate politically. Yet where people are unequal, as in their productive capacity or in their basketball talent, justice requires they be dealt with on their merits. This modified form of the merit test satisfies our earlier point, which suggested that a pure merit test is enormously vulnerable to accepting drastic political and legal inequalities—injustices, we might say. It also meets the criticism that the merit theory never demonstrates sufficient respect for what is due to people as people, regardless of what they do, regardless of their acquired characteristics, and natural strengths.

What is Due to Us Determined by Equality

The egalitarian position holds justice demands that all of us be treated equally because we are all equal members of the human race. The thrust is toward a vast expansion of the situations in which people should be accorded identical treatment, especially in the areas of incomes, status, and social conditions—"social justice." Supporters of the equality test claim that only this direction adheres to the ideal of respect for individual persons, regardless of their varied talents and backgrounds. They contend that if we genuinely respect people, we must respect them regardless of eveything else except their very personhood. They argue that the humblest worker and the greatest captain of industry, the most ruthless academic entrepreneur and the most devoted college teacher are the same in what should count in life—their common humanity—and therefore each should get the same honor and income, as well as their present supposedly equal vote and equal courtroom justice.

This egalitarian perspective on justice is radical. It has been the doctrine of many political and economic revolutionaries whose cry for social justice has rung loudly in almost all recent revolutions from the Bolshevik revolution in 1917 to the Cuban revolution of the 1960s. But it has also been the doctrine of many thinkers and activists who are hardly violent revolutionaries, men in

America like Michael Harrington whose "discovery" of poverty in the United States in the 1960s had much to do with the late War on Poverty, and men in Europe like Albert Camus, who saw the dangers of revolutionaries and the impossibility of full equality, but who urged a more egalitarian world.

The egalitarian theory clashes sharply with the merit test of justice that we apply in art, sports, income, and much else in our society, but we should remember that it is hardly entirely foreign to us. It underlies our understanding of what is just in *political life*, where we believe each should count as one and only one. Even outside of strictly political relationships, egalitarian justice may appeal to us whenever we begin to wonder about the great inequalities around us and ask if their existence is just.

At the least, everyone must contemplate the gap between equality and merit justice and wonder which is right. We certainly cannot forget that merit justice has substantial weaknesses, as egalitarians are quick to point out, especially its tendency to call social and economic relationships just that may have more to do with differences in natural gifts or family environment than anything else. The drawbacks to an egalitarian concept of justice, however, are weighty in their own right. Egalitarians tend to assume that things can be divided up into fair shares in this world. Some, like income, theoretically can be, but all jobs are not going to be equally good, all farmland equally rich, all schools equally effective. Some worry that egalitarians do not understand the costs that would be involved in the massive income redistribution that would be required in the United States or Western Europe to begin to approach their goal. Would the typical, relatively peaceful political system survive such a dramatic experiment? A third pragmatic doubt derives from the ancient dilemma between an equally divided but fixed pie versus an unequally divided but steadily increasing pie, with greater slices for all or almost all. Critics of egalitarian justice fear that as an economic policy it will eliminate economic incentives and thus actually deny the increased life chances that could be ensured if there were income differentials to spur the most creative and productive forward. What is the advantage if we are equal in poverty?

These pragmatic criticisms of the egalitarian approach to social justice are common, but egalitarians insist that they are not fatal to their position. They deny the pessimistic prognosis for radical change that their opponents often make, and they never fail to remind their critics of what they consider to be the enormous human costs of the present inegalitarian social and economic arrangements. They also deny that problems of dividing goods as well as finding nonmonetary incentives in a more egalitarian society are insoluble. They tend to be optimistic about what humans can do. They also point out that pragmatic objections to their ideal theory of justice are not the same thing as objections in principle. Even if pragmatic points prove to have weight, they insist, the worth of the moral ideal of egalitarianism would remain unaffected.

There are more theoretical worries about the egalitarian standard. For example, how far would even the most devoted defender of the equality theory of justice take the ideal? Would anyone seriously suggest that justice existed if we were all equally tortured? Would we claim it just if we were all robbed, as long as we all lost an equal amount? Would it be a just polity if we all surrendered our political rights to the same extent? Justice surely does not mean equality in things that somehow violate the formal standard of due respect to all.

Another objection derives from a confusion for which egalitarians are often responsible. Critics ask whether egalitarians seriously mean to give everyone equal incomes, regardless of the size of their families, their particular medical problems, or other varying needs. In fact, too many egalitarians talk about equality as if they do indeed mean that everyone should receive an identical income. This tone derives partly from the egalitarian attacks on the enormous inequalities to be found everywhere in modern societies, a tone that may seem to suggest that their solution is strict formal equality.

There is no doubt of the egalitarians' belief in equality, of course, but when one examines their argument closely, one finds that rarely do they favor a rigid, formal equality apart from needs. Instead, most egalitarians define equality as an ideal that seeks to make each of us equal in the fundamental aspects of life by distributing income, health care, and the like according to our necessarily differing, individual needs, so that we have real-life equality rather than a formal equality that is often inequality.

What Is Due To Us Determined By Need

Karl Marx was the famous exponent of need as justice. In the nineteenth century his vision of the social order in *The Gotha Program* provided for distribution to "each according to his needs."

The need approach is a form of the egalitarian position, because the needs in question are ordinarily understood as universal to all people, and those whose needs are not met are held to lack the equal respect due to all people. This notion of justice today is applied in many places where the name Karl Marx has never been heard and in ways that have nothing to do with what he would like or appreciate. It lies, for example, behind the minimum-wage law or the provision of welfare payments to the poor in a host of regimes, capitalist or socialist. Proponents of both policies believe that poorly paid workers, or the poor in general, do not receive just treatment if their level of existence falls short of our notions of what is fitting for all human beings—the need definition of justice.

Proponents of the need criterion believe that equality means equal fulfillment of needs that necessarily are unequal among different people in different times. The needs of a bachelor and those of the head of a household of five are obviously not the same, and genuine equality will require quite different incomes in the two cases. Similarly, the education needs of two children who are equally bright but differ tremendously in self-confidence will vary greatly. The student without self-confidence will require far more attention in order to obtain an equal education.

Need must be taken seriously as a view of justice, for it is more effective than formal equality in accomplishing their joint goal—substantive equality. It is also convincing in its belief that if justice concerns rendering what is due to people, we must measure those claims in terms of actual human needs. Yet, as with all theories of justice, there are problems. For one thing, many needs may be hard to satisfy. This is especially true with such psychic needs as love or belonging. Even economic needs cannot be met except in societies with considerable abundance, and where needs exceed what is available to distribute, need cannot solve problems of distributive justice. Second, in any society there will be needs, powerful needs, that some individuals will have but that few of us will want fulfilled. Do we want to assist the compulsive murderer or rapist to fulfill their dangerous needs?

The problem here is the definition of an authentic need. Clearly need is a vague and elastic concept. There is no self-evident definition of what need means for people in common or individual terms. Nor does it appear possible to arrive at some magical solution by uncovering a scientific definition of human needs, for what people need is a normative question that depends on what goals people seek. Even elementary needs like food or shelter depend on the acceptance of the normative goal of life, something many thousands of suicides reject each year.

One way to come to terms with what need should be is to distinguish so-called basic needs from the rest of human needs. While basic needs are not intuitively obvious either, if we adopt the objective of the maintenance of a functioning life as our basic value, we can select those needs whose absence would cause unmistakable harm to people. These would include adequate food, shelter, clothes, and medical care. Agreement that everyone ought to have these things is widespread throughout the world today and illustrates the vitality of the need conception of justice. Thoroughgoing enthusiasts for the need test, however, want to go far beyond a minimum-needs theory of justice. Hope for any agreement on criteria fades before varying individual preferences. Nor can we blink at the possibility that varying needs may bring social and interpersonal conflicts. I may "need" peace and quiet and you may "need" to practice your electric guitar. It will not always be possible to reconcile our differences. The fact remains, also, that even in rich nations many noneconomic needs simply cannot be satisfied.

Critics of a need theory of justice also worry about another problem. As with a formal egalitarian concept of justice, they fear that the need test may fail to provide incentives for people to continue working, without which no society can long endure and few personal needs met. Who will bother to work if people's needs are fulfilled without working? Advocates of the need approach hope that people will go on working, or can be convinced to do so, for community goals or personal satisfaction. These alternative incentives can make a difference, but whether they can make enough of a difference is at the least questionable.

TOWARD RESOLUTION

Each of the theories of justice we have examined has its attractions and each has considerable plausibility. Each has a place when we envision justice in one situation or another. All of them are fallible, however, and none seems to us able to stand alone as a complete theory of justice. This reality provides us with the clue toward a resolution of a satisfactory definition of justice. It tells us that some combination of ideas of justice promises to bring us closer to our goal of a defensible theory of justice. We want to argue, specifically, that need, utility, equality, and merit all have valid associations with the norms and contexts of justice. Though we believe need is justice's most important single element, even it cannot stand alone any more effectively than the others. Yet need, more than a strict and formalistic equality, comes closest to justice understood as rendering what is due to us as human persons. Only need allows for the fact that to achieve substantive equality among human beings and thus equal respect, we will have to afford different services and different degrees of service to individuals.

Yet need must be modified as a norm of justice by three other principles. It should be watched over by social utility, which we may elect to consider a standard of justice. A concept of the general public good, such as the value of life, will be necessary in order to select among competing needs, to deny clearly antisocial needs, such as the "needs" of pathological murderers, and to guard against the abuse of legitimate needs, such as is perpetrated by hypochondriacs.

The standard of strict equality must also modify need in the case of political influence. Equal political opportunity may be hard to achieve, but it should be defended as a goal, in that politics should serve people and not the reverse. Equality should also be maintained in the application of laws in and out of the courtroom. This, too, is at the very heart of the democratic faith that celebrates each man and woman as members of the human race.

Finally, there is little doubt that despite its flaws, merit plays a large part in our normal, linguistic perceptions of justice. There is no reason why it should not continue to be our operational standard of justice in numerous private areas of life, from baseball rules to artistic recognition. In politics or social policy we doubt that it can legitimately serve as a substitute for a needs standard without vitiating our argument that justice must, above all, involve respect for all of us as human beings, regardless of our accidental talents or backgrounds. In the economic realm merit must be taken seriously, both for practical reasons and because of the importance of honoring the differences that are as much a part of all of us as what we share in common. Thus there should probably be a merit feature to income distribution as well. We must, however, have a vigorous and concerned welfare state to speak to people's basic needs for life and education, even if we decide on a merit system of income distribution thereafter.

Our conclusion is that no single formula explains justice properly. Justice has several sides, and several different visions of justice must be included in an adequate understanding of the word. We do not claim we have solved all the ancient riddles that surround the nature of justice. Our point has been to illustrate the many common images of justice that we employ, to explain the meaning, implications, strengths, and weaknesses of each view and to stimulate thought about this concept we use so often. Wrestling with justice is like trying to climb a greased pole. Yet politics is too often concerned with justice for any of us to seek to escape this climb.

SUGGESTIONS FOR SUPPLEMENTARY READING

General

Brandt, R., Ed. *Social Justice*. Englewood Cliffs, N.J.: Prentice-Hall, 1962.
Olafsen, F., Ed. *Justice and Social Policy*. Englewood Cliffs, N.J.: Prentice-Hall, 1961.
Walzer, M. *Spheres of Justice*. New York: Basic Books, 1983.

Divine and Natural Justice

Aristotle. *The Politics*. Many editions.
Pieper, J. *Justice*. New York: Pantheon Books, 1955.
Plato. *The Republic*. Many editions.
Sumner, W. G. *Social Darwinism*. Englewood Cliffs, N.J.: Prentice-Hall, 1963.

Procedural and Legalistic Justice

Fuller, L. *The Morality of Law*. New Haven: Yale University Press, 1965.
Kelsen, Hans. *What Is Justice?* Berkeley: University of California Press, 1957.

Utilitarianism

Barry, B. *The Liberal Theory of Justice: A Critical Examination of the Principal Doctrines of A Theory of Justice by John Rawls*. Clarendon: Oxford University Press, 1973.
Bentham, Jeremy. *The Principles of Morals and Legislation*. Many publications.
Mill, John Stuart. *Utilitarianism*. New York: Dutton, 1951.
Rawls, John. *A Theory of Justice*. Cambridge, Mass.: Harvard University Press, 1971.

Merit, Equality, Need

Bedau, Hugo, Ed. *Justice and Equality*. Englewood Cliffs, N.J.: Prentice-Hall, 1971.

Benn, S. I. and Peters, R. S. *The Principles of Political Thought.* New York: Free Press, 1959.
Cahn, E. *The Sense of Injustice.* New York: New York University Press, 1949.
Ginsberg, M. *On Justice in Society.* Baltimore, Md.: Penguin Books, 1965.
Marx, Karl. *Critique of the Gotha Program.* Many editions.

7

Political Obligation

Political obligation concerns what duties citizens owe to the political system in which they live and what duties it owes to them. It includes the issue of when obedience or disobedience to a political community is morally appropriate. Whenever we ask "Should I obey this law?" or "Do I have a right to disobey my government?" or "When am I obligated to the political community in which I live?" we confront the issue. Our individual answers to these important questions constitute our own theory of political obligation. Moreover, our answers, no matter how simple or how complicated, are part of a tradition of concern about the question. It began with Socrates facing death in the Athens of the early fourth century, B.C. and lives on today, as thoughtful people puzzle over their obligations to the state and its obligations to them.

We have every reason to believe that in the future there will be no end of occasions in which people find themselves confronted with agonizing decisions regarding their political obligations. Recent years have seen many examples of difficult challenges posed to ethical obedience or disobedience to the state. For example, many draft-aged men self-consciously faced the problems of political obligation in the Vietnam War. Others face similar, though muted, problems with the draft registration requirements of the 1980s. The several thousands of young men who fled to Canada or who went to jail rather than serve in Vietnam, plus many more who elected to serve in the army, did the best they could to work out a personal answer. While their conclusions differed, anyone in American colleges in those years remembers the endless, intense discussions—discussions whose consequences are now a permanent part of American history.

This recent experience in our own history suggests what will always be true: that war is especially likely to test political loyalties and to stimulate thought on the subject of political obligation. Loyalty and obligation in wartime affect people directly, sometimes demanding their lives, and it is hardly surprising that the possibility of losing one's life stimulates philosophical reflection. In the past, war was often the setting for statements of political obligation. The English civil war of the seventeenth century was the context for Thomas Hobbes's classic defense of political obedience. Edmund Burke's conservative theory of obligation was written in an England he believed to be endangered by the revolutionary France of the late eighteenth century. War has also, however, brought forth energetic denials of political obligation, as we remember when we think of Thoreau in jail for refusing to acknowledge any obligation to support our government in the Mexican-American War (which he contended was fought to promote the evils of slavery) or of the multitude of pacifists in human history who chose to disobey their governments rather than kill. War is both the pacifist's and the patriot's hour.

In or out of wars, it has also been true that groups as well as individuals have faced crises that raise the issue of political obligation. From the problems the first Christians faced with imperial Rome until now, an obvious case in point has been the clash between religious movements or churches and their respective political communities. Consider the conflict in the United States between Christian fundamentalists who have wished to educate their own children and the states that denied them this "right," the ongoing protest of pacifist Quakers who resist draft legislation, or the great struggle in the late nineteenth century between the polygamist Mormons and a monogamist state and society. All of these conflicts have produced disobedience and all have challenged reigning concepts of political obligation.

They also demonstrate that moral perplexities over adherence to laws or governments often occur in situations in which there are multiple obligations. Moral life in the state as elsewhere can be complex. One may be pulled in many directions by commitment to religion, family, friends, principles, or state. When these multiple commitments do not join to reinforce the demands of a political order, then the strength or ultimately the validity of one's customary sense of political obligation may be undermined and then tested. So it has been sometimes with the Amish, Quakers, Mormons, and countless others.

Political obligation also looms up when groups seek to be included in a political order. Much of the black civil rights movement has illustrated the fact that repeated denials of political obligation, considerable civil disobedience, and other assaults on the political order can derive from a desire for equal rights in a political system. Martin Luther King, Jr., often talked in terms of the appropriate conditions of political obedience and disobedience, as he sought to press the case for blacks in American life. From one angle too, the American Civil War was a battle over political obligation, over whether slaves should be citizens, with political rights and obligations, as well as over the secessionists' belief that they owed no obligation to the government of the United States.

Another obligation dilemma rooted in a group framework is posed by the experiences of prisoners of war. While American prisoners of war in Vietnam generally remained committed to their political obligation to the United States, while not jeopardizing obligations they had to their fellow prisoners or their families at home, this was often not the experience of American POWs in the Korean War. Extensive collaboration took place in Korea, due to a combination of severe conditions of imprisonment, loyalty to other prisoners, concern about families, and selfish expediency. That some of the collaboration in Korea occurred in return for messages sent to the prisoners' families in the United States, or simply to get out alive, poignantly indicated how multiple obligations can often lead to a crisis in political obligation.

Conflict and tension over political obligation also arise in situations involving entire peoples, especially in the cases of colonial or conquered peoples. An examination of the colonial literature before the American Revolution affords a fascinating example of the process by which one people reluctantly challenged their relationship with their founding nation. From 1765 to 1776 colonial pamphleteers moved from the status of increasingly discontented but still loyal citizens to a stance that denied any political obligation to Britain—a dramatic and drastic alteration of their views. This process has been simpler but no less dramatic for peoples seeking self-determination more recently, such as the host of former British, French, or Belgian colonies in Africa. With some exceptions, Third World theorists had never acknowledged any political obligation to their imperial rulers. Consequently, they had a shorter intellectual road to travel to rebellion. In the end, however, many of their arguments were quite similar to those of the American revolutionary thinkers. They too stressed that colonial peoples should be free of rulers to whom they owed no moral allegiance or political obligation.

In short, from the day Socrates had to decide whether he was obligated enough to the Athenian state to give up his life at its command until now, the issue of political obligation has faced individuals, groups, and indeed, entire nations.

GENERAL CHARACTERISTICS OF POLITICAL OBLIGATION

As with any truly serious matter, political obligation is not simple, nor is it something upon which everyone agrees. While there are different concepts of political obligation, which we will explore, most discussions begin, as ours must, with a basic understanding of what political obligation in most of its forms involves. First, we must be clear from the start that political obligation has to do with ethics, with what is morally right. Whether that obligation is practical or impractical, convenient or inconvenient, is secondary to the standard of right that underlies a given theory of political obligation. Some views link political obligation to human desires, others to natural laws, still others to contracts made, but all agree that the matter is ethical.

Second, political obligation has to do with what one must owe (or must refuse to owe) to a political community. It may or may not derive from choices made, as we will see, but what it involves is a demand that must be honored. It is about mustness, about what one has to do to be ethical, not necessarily about what one desires to do. This is why it is so frightening a concept, especially in cultures such as ours, in which individual choice and freedom are so attractive. Obligation, including political obligation, says that if one is obligated, then one must obey, regardless of one's preference, and that should always give each of us pause.

A third dimension of political obligation is that it occurs only in situations of mutuality, when there are people with whom one may conceivably be in moral contact. Obviously Robinson Crusoe, when he was apparently alone on his desert isle, had no political duties. More important, mutuality means that there can be no condition of political owing where there is no political community, or when members of a state refuse to agree that they are connected with each other in a manner that mandates obedience under certain conditions. This spirit of mutuality at some level is basic for the existence of political obligation, because without at least some sense of national, racial, ethnic, or ethical respect among people, genuine moral relations make little sense. Nations are like organizations—they die when their people no longer care for them and their members, or they eke out a morally empty existence under the reign of the sword or spy.

Finally, many concepts of obligation suggest that genuine political obligation must be a reciprocal, even egalitarian relationship. While this was not always true, for example in feudal society, obligation is not generally viewed today as limited to one group in society, nor as having different ethical weights among otherwise equal citizens, but as a duty that we owe to each other as equal citizens. U.S. citizens, for example, do not normally have differing political duties as citizens nor, in theory, do the nationals of most other countries who share the modern belief that citizenship implies a fundamental equality in rights and duties. One of the most common complaints of men who received their draft notices in the Vietnam years was that young men were being asked to fight a war made by old men. This was an echo of the idea that political duties should be shared equally by all. It posed a serious objection to the draft then and it still does, unless all men (and perhaps women, too) have to serve at one time or another.

THEORIES OF POLITICAL OBLIGATION

When we speak of political obligation, we are talking about the relationship between citizens and their political order, an ethical relationship, existing at its best in an atmosphere of mutuality and equality. Yet this brings us only to the threshold of this important topic. Knowing what is involved in general in the concept of political obligation is by no means the same thing as considering which form is the best. It is this second issue that is the heart of the matter for us. It must be answered if we are to make headway in our search for a moral basis on which to reply to the ongoing human query, When should I obey; when should I disobey?

Since the subject is so important, it is not surprising that there have been many responses to the quest for the ideal understanding of political obligation, its demands, and its limits. Five theories illuminate most clearly the serious issues at stake. Some of these, such as consent and benefit theory are familiar to many Americans, but we must not ignore others—natural-law, tradition, and group concepts—lest we fail to observe the full range of alternatives debated in the history of political obligation.

Natural Law

Natural-law thinkers argue that in order to decide when one should obey, each of us must look at the truths of the broader moral universe in which we dwell. They provide boundaries for political obligation from a standard higher than any that may be developed by individual consent, the wishes of a political majority, or personal or social benefit. Their higher standard is usually divine law, though sometimes it refers to nature apart from any god. In either case, the assumption is that these higher laws set the terms for human ethical relationships, including political obligation.

Throughout history the exact content of these binding natural laws, as they apply to political obedience or disobedience, has varied. In the Western world, the common view has been that natural and divine law counseled obedience by the citizen to the political order. This was what the divine laws taught Socrates in ancient Athens; this was the central message of traditional Christianity in the hands of St. Paul or St. Augustine, and it was the view of our duty of the leading American Tory theorist at the time of our revolution, Jonathan Boucher. All agreed that God, or the gods, commanded the duty of loyalty to the state. While there might be some limits, the main political injunction was "render unto Caesar." This was a profoundly conservative theory of political obligation.

Yet other versions of divinely grounded natural laws have led in different directions. Martin Luther King, Jr., believed that Christian natural law prohibited obedience to any state that failed to treat all persons equally, a position that many abolitionists, including Thoreau, Garrison, and John Brown had argued a century earlier in the debate over slavery. The implication of their understanding of divine law was hardly conservative. Oftentimes, in fact, natural law has been the basis for political revolution. This is the doctrine of our own Declaration of Independence, which proclaims that the Creator has ordained the natural right to "life, liberty, and the pursuit of happiness" and that a regime that denies these rights must be replaced.

The frequent recourse to natural (or divine) standards to define political obligation is not so self-evident an approach, however, as to be invulnerable to criticism. One objection follows from the multitude of contending versions of the content of a higher truth that is supposedly absolute and without question. It asks whether the existence of these alternative perspectives helps anybody in resolving dilemmas of political obligation, even as it surely reveals a miasma of confusion both about the nature of the laws of God and what their implications might be for political duty. The moral cacophony of competing truths we meet in human experience only seems to promote the idea that there is no single answer, even though one or another may still be true. Moreover, ours is a skeptical age. To be sure, many people are religious, and find their standards for obligation and much else in their religion. This is true in all sorts of places of the world, from India to Iran to the United States. Many others, however, find absolute natural-law standards, religious or otherwise, weakened or gone in the face of contemporary skepticism.

There is also a troubling and peculiar overconfidence among many proponents of natural law, that if there were standards on which everyone could agree, this fact would help us in concrete moral and political decisions. Yet broad principles, no mater how "natural" or "divine," do not easily translate into specifics. For example, Christians have never been able to agree as to the concrete meaning of the Old Testament injunction "Thou shalt not kill." Does this commandment forbid wars? Leading Catholic thinkers like St. Augustine and St. Thomas repeatedly denied this interpretation, while Quakers and Mennonites defend it. Does this rule forbid capital punishment? Most Christian thinkers, before and after the Inquisition have not thought so, yet others have eloquently disagreed.

Despite these substantial problems, however, today there remain vibrant traditions in political theory that continue to insist that religion-based natural law must be the ultimate recourse in questions of political duty. Some people still very much believe in the existence and/or the value of absolute truth in political and ethical discourse. It may be a matter of faith, but the faith is still alive for some followers of Martin Luther King, Jr., of William F. Buckley, Jr., of other American conservatives, and of radicals such as the Berrigan brothers in the Catholic Left.

History and Tradition

A second approach to the puzzle of political obligation focuses on the moral weight of historical traditions. Sympathizers with this view argue that what is customary or traditional in a society should determine the boundaries of political obligation for its citizens. For them, human experience articulated in tradition is a sounder guide than any temporary majority sentiment, elusive natural law, or individual opinion. Edmund Burke, the eighteenth-century British thinker, best articulated this argument. To him society was a contract between the past, the present, and the future, in which all of us were bound together in human custom and experience. To ignore these ties of social history, to ignore our commitments to the past, was immoral.

Burke's argument appeared as an attack on the French Revolution, which explicitly rejected a Burkean notion of traditional definitions of political obligation, but it continues to be employed today by many American conservatives in an obviously different environment, often in conjunction with a religious natural-law stance. More broadly, it is the characteristic of ardent patriots in every land who are proud of their country, its accomplishments, and its past.

In political terms, thinkers who employ a traditionalist argument usually conclude that the parameters of political obligation are broad and the bounds of morally permissible disobedience narrow. History, it would seem, usually teaches obedience, although, in fact, what the past may be said to teach encompasses many different things. History can provide a basis for political disobligation, as the Huguenots of France, the American colonists of England, or the Leninist sufferers under the Czars perceived from their own histories. Our point is that history is a record of many things, and the interpreter's viewpoint usually defines its essence.

The main problem with this approach to political obligation, however, is not the dubious possibility of determining what a tradition says, although this is no modest difficulty. The greater problem is that there is no particular reason to assume that just because something has been done in a certain way in the past, it ought to be done that way in the future. Why does it follow that because your father served in the military you are obligated to do so? What is there that is specifically moral about the past? It may be moral or it may not be. So with customary understandings of one's political duties and obligations; they may be ethical or they may not be, but their antiquity decides nothing.

This does not imply that we cannot learn a good deal from the past. We can and we should. Yet the existence or nonexistence of an obligation cannot stand or fall merely because it is traditional (or previously unknown). An argument must be made, as is done, for example, by a pragmatic case for obligation which stresses that following the past is valuable for specific reasons, such as an encouragement of a stable society.

Consent

In our age, in our nation, neither natural or divine laws nor the plea for the past have been the most familiar basis of political obligation. It is consent that is the usual approach—as it has long been. American revolutionary times were filled with phrases such as "no taxation without representation" and "consent of the governed." Many revolutions since then have repeated the idea that citizens owe political obligations to a state only so long as it is based on the will of its citizens, stipulating that they may overthrow any political order that fails to adhere to its duty. Today virtually all governments in the world claim that their foundations lie in popular consent. It is routine for governments, including ours, to invoke their alleged popular support as the justification for demanding that laws be obeyed and institutions honored. At the same time, revolutionary movements continue to use consent arguments to buttress their drive to remove regimes in power, as current insurgent groups in Central America illustrate so well. Many American black activists or draft-age Americans during the Vietnam War also maintained that they were excluded from the process of consent in America and therefore owed nothing to the political order. All of these examples attest to the continuing vitality of consent in the councils of human thinking about political obligation.

The contemporary tendency to settle political-obligation disputes by invoking the magic concept of consent should not mislead us into the belief that consent is a simple notion, uniformly interpreted and applied. The truth is the opposite, and the popularity of the appeal of consent derives to a large extent from the fact that consent has meant so many contrasting things to thinkers and has had equally varying implications in concrete crises of political obligation. Many of the most intense disputes about political obligation today accept the idea that consent is the only proper theory of political obligation, but people strongly disagree over the meaning of consent, especially as it applies to their own concrete situation. Our first practical and intellectual problem with a consent-based theory of obligation, then, is to determine a good answer to the question of the meaning of consent.

There are many possible answers, but the most obvious definition of consent is direct consent, the idea that people are politically obligated only if they have taken a formal, legal, and public oath of allegiance to a given political system. It is evident that few people in the world are called on to take such an oath, but it is equally evident that it would be easy in most nations to meet the standards of direct consent. All a country would need is a regularized process for citizens to take periodic oaths of consent, perhaps at local post offices. Loyalty oaths of varying descriptions now exist for inductees into the U.S. armed forces, for many teachers, and for elected public officials, among others, and they cause little or no comment or challenge.

The real problem with the direct-consent test is not so much whether it now exists, or could be easily made available, as whether its inherent directness disqualifies it as a justifiable act leading to political commitment. Signing a statement or declaring something on oath is too formalistic and too insubstantial an action in terms of the lives of most of us to carry the enormous consequences that political obligation may require, including military service. Deep and abiding consent can scarcely be measured except by intense action or long-term choice, neither of which most forms of direct consent promote. It is quite plausible, as has often been the case with loyalty oaths, that citizens could go through the motions of "consenting" as routinely as they apply for their new license plates—and with as little implied commitment. Probably few citizens would have to be coerced in most situations to give direct consent, but few also would probably believe they had given much of anything.

The resulting paradox is that, though direct consent appears to be the sturdiest and most moral form of political obligation, it is actually one of the worst. This paradox has long been perceived by political thinkers, few of whom agreed with Senator McCarthy and his allies in the 1950s that loyalty oaths would measure loyalty or expose Communists.

Most consent advocates advance the more considered view that genuine consent is best demonstrated by residence, or by political participation, or at least the opportunity to participate. This type of consent may be termed indirect or tacit consent. Its supporters argue that selected measures of tacit consent, while less immediate than direct consent, are actually much more substantial indicators of consent. As we will see, their critics are suspicious, contending that proponents of tacit consent are more concerned to establish a moral basis for claiming that people are obligated and must obey than they are to defend the moral right of individual choice (consent).

A famous theorist of tacit consent was the seventeenth-century Englishman John Locke, who maintained that it was perfectly proper to believe that a person was politically obligated if he had lived in a country, traveled its highways, or perhaps inherited property under its laws. This classic view suggested that residence implied consent, assuming it was possible to leave. Many countries including our own more or less consciously employ this standard of consent, but it seems as empty in its own peculiar manner as is direct consent. Even if consent is to be indirect, mere residence scarcely suggests anything definite as a token of consent, unless the word consent carries no meaning of active, aware choice. Certainly some people proudly proclaim that their residence in a country is proof of their chosen loyalty to it and of their willingness to accept political obligation in its cause. There is little doubt, however, that for many others residence is an accident of birth or circumstance more than a choice, and emigration represents an unrealistic alternative. The trouble with "Love it or leave it" is that a great many people fall into neither camp and should not be forced to do so.

Participation tests do compensate for this weakness by insisting that there must be action for there to be consent and thus obligation. Yet if we use the measure of political participation, we reach the conclusion that most Americans are not obligated. If we take the most widespread category of political activity, voting in presidential elections, almost 50 percent of the adult population would seem to be nonconsenting, despite the fact that public-opinion polls show that few citizens feel nonobligated. Matters are complicated by the fact that voting for president once every four years hardly constitutes a measure of consent with any more depth or length of intensity than direct consent provides. Yet we know that only about 5 percent of the population participates in politics in any more active manner than by casting an occasional vote. And the fact remains that since a low degree of participation does not appear to affect, much less undermine, the ordinary American's sense of political obligation, the inability of the political participation test to tap this sentiment amounts to a serious flaw.

Another form of the participation test marks the opportunity to participate politically as the appropriate requirement for political obligation. It holds that if people have a roughly equal chance with their fellow citizens to affect the policies of their government, whether or not they choose to exercise that right, then they should be obligated to support the political order. This test also insists that the citizen, of course, must understand that political obligation will be the consequence of political opportunity. Few societies, including our own, approach the goal of roughly equal opportunity, but the objective is possible, especially as public financing of campaigns is adopted. The test also mandates that for there to be valid choice, a realistic opportunity for citizens to leave a country must be made available.

A serious problem here, though, is the bind in which minorities, especially consistently losing minorities, may find themselves in a political system where consent and obligation are tied to various political participation standards. Even if minorities have the right to participate (and do so), they could find themselves obligated to their own oppression, if not to the extent of the loss of their political rights. Depending on the nature of the minority, they might, for example, get no policy benefits although heavily taxed, or they might experience severe social discrimination. While they might emigrate, this change of life is never easy, nor is it clear why they should have to leave more than anyone else.

Many thinkers accuse the proponents of consent via the test of political participation opportunities of promoting a theory devoted more to order than to justice. The theory seems to insist that disadvantaged minorities are obligated, no matter what, unless they emigrate, leaving little room for civil disobedience or other tactics that might be followed by citizens who reject their political obligation, yet still love their country or home. Critics say that the opportunity test, like all the other tacit or indirect tests, thus shows that its true interest is in getting obedience rather than respecting the individual (or group). This criticism motivates one last variety of consent, which concludes that most types of consent-based theories of political obligation are indeed ill-concealed maneuvers to pry out of people a moral commitment without genuine consent. This form, advanced by Hannah Pitkin, might be termed the "deserved" test, because it argues that one is obligated to a government only when its form and/or its policies hypothetically would merit or deserve consent if a citizen were asked about them. The test tries to provide as much meaningful choice as possible by substituting for direct or indirect consent an ongoing process in which individuals decide their obligation to their government or its policies whenever and as often as they choose. Proponents contend that here at last is a standard—deserved consent—that really provides generous choice, the generous choice they contend must be present before one can say someone is obligated through consent.

Pitkin's deserved consent raises an important issue too often neglected by other variants of consent. It insists that it is important to decide not merely the standards that constitute consent, but also what it is one consents to (or dissents from). Of course, individuals disagree about what governments and policies merit consent, but Pitkin's point is that these matters must play a role in deciding whether one consents or not. Can it ever be legitimate to consent to one's enslavement? Can one ever consent to a political system in which one is part of a consistently losing minority? These queries highlight the suggestion that consent may be structured by government and its actions, as well as by individual choices.

Yet the problems with this attractive theory are many. The deserved theory makes too much of conscious judgment and overrationalizes human behavior; it would likely have the practical effect of ensuring the obligation of the less-educated and/or the less aware. It also leaves too much to present individual choice, allowing people to decide by their own standards whether a government is satisfactory, with no guaranteed attention either to community judgments or to past decisions. The individual may not be right by "objective" criteria, but he or she alone will decide. The evaluation of an individual's moral correctness is either left to outside observers who care to evaluate such things for their own reasons or to the interplay of citizens and their ideas within a polity. This is so true that the skeptic of the Pitkin test can only wonder if it is about political obligation or virtual philosophical anarchism, the denial of the possibility of obligation. For many citizens surely this would not take place; in any society many, perhaps too many, are all too willing to declare their consent. In practical terms, however, it is certainly legitimate to wonder whether many other citizens would declare they were not obligated whenever it was convenient for them. The result could be a government that could not govern because it could not collect enough taxes or because it could not raise an army —even if most citizens supported their political community in a general way.

Somewhere between the tacit-consent theories, which are so concerned to justify political obligation that they almost eliminate consent, and those so concerned about consent that they offer governments little chance to obtain morally sanctioned obedience except when there are no costs to the citizen, there must be a better solution within the popular framework of consent theory. Yet it has not appeared amid the myriad contenders for that honor.

Group Theory

A somewhat more subtle obligation theory than consent is the group concept, which derives political obligation from group memberships or interactions. Its proponents contend that one or several groups are the center of every person's moral universe, structuring all obligations and consequently determining our duties, including our duties to a political community. Examples might include one's family, friends, religious group, political organization, and among some people the political community itself. The idea is that such group connections, when they are based in intense, deep, emotional bonds, are and should be what we really care about and what we really feel count most with us in life. In comparison with them consent seems formal and superficial. Even in situations where an obligation is generally acknowledged to exist by consent, as in a marriage contract, group theorists argue that the true basis for the obligation that marriage partners feel toward each other lies in their emotional bonding. Marriages die, they point out, not when people get divorced; rather people get divorced when emotional bonding has died.

The Party as a Group

Lenin's famous revolutionary pamphlet *What Is To Be Done?* (1902) is justly renowned for its explicit and detailed theory of the action-oriented revolutionary socialist party. It is also fascinating for its group concept of obligation in a political world. It is an apt example of the view that obligation in politics is built on an intense, intimate set of interactions among members of a group who give everything to their cause and each other. This gift of commitment to the party determines all else in their lives, including their attitude toward the larger political order around them. The party is first—indeed, the party is everything.

An impressive—or frightening—example of this version of group obligation may be seen in Bertoldt Brecht's play *The Measures Taken* (1930), in which the Young Comrade is killed by his associates, the Four Agitators, because he would not surrender his moral individuality to the dictates of his group—in his case, the Communist party. It defined obligation for its individual members. It admonished its members, "Do not see with your own eyes! . . . all of you are nameless and motherless, blank pages on which the revolution writes its instructions."

Such a notion of group obligation is unattractive for a number of weighty reasons, but it is its exclusiveness that makes the least sense with either normative or empirical analysis. A view that defines the moral world of the committed, as the Russian anarchist Nechayev did in 1868 in his *Catechism of the Revolutionist*, as one in which the dedicated "has no personal interest, no affairs, sentiments, attachments, property. . . . Everything in him is absorbed by one exclusive interest, one thought, one passion" hardly respects the myriad moral duties that most people reasonably want to and do assume. People choose to have multiple obligations, with their political order as well as with friends, family, or more than one organization, for a variety of reasons, no doubt, but they do make the choice for a complex moral world time and again.

The Group as a Participatory Community

A more common version of the group basis for political obligation wants to think about the general political community as a group and to suggest that order is composed of a community of participatory citizens who are about equal in political power; they owe each other a political loyalty that is ethical in implication. This is the treasured objective of participatory democrats in all ages. Their hope is that such a society will be so equal in its social and economic features that political equality will be more than the rhetorical phrase it usually is. Their trust is that people, confident of their relative equality, will actively work together in molding a practical, caring community. Their aspiration is a political order in which significant amounts of power will be sharply decentralized to small local units of government, since only there can community have a fighting chance to flourish and endure.

Sympathetic contemporary theorists of this ideal insist that while people must choose to live in this order, it is not so much their consent to do so that is the basis of their political obligation as the individual's activity with others in a living, participatory political order. The idea is that sharing among active, involved members of a participatory community necessarily creates bonds among its members, bonds that create obligation to the entire community. The assumption is that these bonds will be at least in part emotional in origin and will run deeper into people's being than any merely formal, rational obligation arrangements. They will also be much more immediate than consent relations to a distant and cold state can be.

Many participatory democrats do not believe that obligation problems are likely to arise in an ideal participatory society. For them obligations will be real and intense, as only group bonding can be. Their society will not fear that in times of trouble or crisis it cannot count on the support of its obligated members. The problem, however, is why participatory democrats of this sort, or any group-based theorists of obligation, believe that close group interaction produces obligations. Why does participation create obligation? In this case, why would participation in a direct democracy mean that the citizens would owe each other political obligation?

The Group as a Natural Solidarity

The question arises even more sharply for those who propose that the most important group-based obligations relevant to politics are those derived from "natural" solidarity. Some Marxists talk of the working class in language that implies that because all workers are workers (participate, so to speak in that category), they owe each other a historical obligation. Some blacks and some whites have contended that racial categories also determine the contours of obligation in a natural and irrevocable sense. A broader appeal has been made to the humanity that all persons share in common. This approach seeks to persuade us that the natural similarity that we all share as persons creates an obligation that must guide us. The obligation to humanity derived from our necessary participation in the human species deductively defines the parameters of our immediate political commitments: Only states that affirm in the reality of their life and policy the ethical demands of the greater natural obligation— equal respect for all human beings—deserve any political obedience or respect. The vision of the Nuremberg trials, the belief that there are "crimes against humanity" that may never be committed, no matter what statist loyalties one may have, is an example of this concept in recent political history. For some modern thinkers, the idea of a supreme obligation to humanity is less a limit on human action than an affirmation of what amounts to a new version of the religion of humanity. Albert Camus, the French existentialist, argued in *The Plague* that the supreme human responsibility is to all mankind and not any single state or political party; the human group matters most of all, and the state is a distant entry on the list of ethical priorities.

The Primary Group and Natural Obligation

Group theories of obligation undoubtedly make most sense to many people when they are put in terms of obligations to primary groups, especially one's family and friends. Such relationships are universal; virtually everyone has some family and friends and there are few people who do not strive to have both or do not consider them natural. Moreover, obligations to one's family and friends are often as intense as any obligations can be, at least as measured by people's feelings. Yet they do not derive in the main from consent arrangements. As in our earlier example of legal marriage, legal consent may exist, but the felt basis for obligation among close family and friends is never legal. It is emotive and all the more powerful for that. Proponents insist that this is, in fact, the model for all other natural-group obligations and it is the best evidence for their pervasive existence.

The political implications of such primary-group obligations are usually clear. They do not rule out obligation to the political community. Nor do they rule out support for the state when it serves to protect and promote group obligations. The suggestion clearly is that for most people the obligations that really count will come from their personal lives, among family and friends, and not the state. Moreover, the potential for conflict with the state will always be present. Whenever it demands obedience on the basis of its obligation claims in a manner that interferes with a citizen's primary obligations, trouble can be expected.

Yet none of these group-based obligations can carry people with them unless they happen to feel these obligations. If you do not feel obligated to your family, it is hard to convince you that you should be. Similarly, only a dedicated liberal humanist is likely to propose that the natural fact that we are all human beings creates an undeniable obligation to humanity, perhaps above all else. The point is that the plausibility of the numerous and sometimes conflicting claims about natural-group obligations depends less on arguments for their validity than on shared (or not shared) feelings of solidarity and obligation. They derive less from the mind and more from the heart, which explains both their frequent power and their frequent invulnerability to rational argument and discussion.

Natural obligation does not really respect the individual rational choosing person. Group obligations are not the product of choice so much as emotions and circumstances. They implicitly reject the model of the individual as a rational free person, which has dominated so much of Western thought. As a result, they are particularly obnoxious to consent theorists. The model of the person that consent thinkers propose is very far from that of group theorists, for whom we are less rational choosing beings than emotive creatures best understood by our complex of social relations that bind us morally, often beyond our will.

Benefit Theory

A fifth and final theory of obligation concerns itself strictly with benefits. It looks at obligation as a payment that citizens make in return for what they obtain from membership in a political order or from following the laws of a particular government. Obedience or resistance ultimately flows from the answer to the old pragmatic question of "What have you done for me lately?" This is a response to problems of obligation that is a common one underlying the enthusiasm many Americans have felt for their political order, although it is also the practical basis for the conviction of other Americans that they owe little to it.

This view is quite close in some features to consent tests that use political or economic participation as their evidence of consent. Yet it differs from such consent criteria because it dispenses with all the elaborate philosophical baggage of consent theory. It simply says, "If I am gaining from the order, I owe it something (obedience) in return, whereas I owe it nothing if I am not gaining from it."

Benefit theories often appeal to us more than others so long as they require that definitions of benefit be both socially concerned and based on agreed stand ards. Critics doubt if it is possible for societies to unite on general standards of benefits, but there is no reason to assume that this is an impossible task. People may well be able to agree on a series of services and rights that could make up a minimum definition of what citizens ought to expect from their political order. And it is an advantage of a benefit theory that it places governments on notice that they exist not by divine or natural right, not because of some dubious, stretched, hard-to-measure "consent," but because (and only if) they assist citizens.

Regimes should operate for our benefit, and when they do not we have no obligation to them. No one, nor any people as a whole, should be embarrassed to ask of government the question, "What have you done for me?" No elaborate philosophical structure concerning consent theory or anything else should drive us from this instrumental view of politics. If a government helps its people by the people's lights, they owe it their allegiance; if it does not, they owe it nothing and indeed they ought to get rid of it.

Critics of the benefit test of obligation protest that all this is a crude and selfish theory of obligation, one that cares only about what gains citizens can get from government. The idea, however, that governments and political communities exist only for the benefit of their citizens is an ethical idea, one of the most stirring and hardwon of all times. To base political obligation on benefit is to affirm the idea that the citizens of a nation are what really matter in politics, and that ultimately only they are the sources of authority.

Others fear that a benefit theory will work out in practice to encourage anarchism. This could happen if the standards of benefit that citizens used to determine their obligation were developed and employed according to individual norms. But benefit theorists almost always insist that the standards that will count, the benefits that must be received before obligation may be incurred, will be decided by the political community as a whole, not by individual judgments. And even in cases where individuals contend that they are not obligated because appropriate benefits have not come to them, their judgment would have to be reviewed by a "neutral" agency to ascertain that this is in fact the case. Indeed, compared to Pitkin's deserved-consent test, the benefit test is quite community minded.

CONCLUSION

While a benefit theory of obligation is attractive, the broader objective of this chapter has been to give some clear idea of the alternative ways in which people have reflected about political obligation and the importance of their reflections. Because this is not a simple matter, it is natural sometimes to pretend we can avoid it. Some undertake to do so by asserting that there is no practical need to worry about how to answer the summons to obedience or disobedience. Most people get along with their government—and most governments with their citizens—if for no other reason than that the weight of every nation's socialization process is brought to bear on the task of ensuring that its citizenry will be obedient men and women. Simple convenience works toward the same end. It is easy to obey and not think about it. The advantage is that as a result one will avoid the police. We also routinely obey because many laws are obviously in our self-interest—stopping at red lights on a busy street, for example. Thus, it may be said, in most cases we have no need of fancy theories of political obligation.

Similarly, the skeptic notes that when people do refuse to follow their government or its rules, the explanation rarely has much to do with theories of obligation. The suspicion once again is that mundane motivations generate disobedience. People go through stop signs, for instance, when they find it necessary in practical terms (as when a mother in childbirth is being rushed to a hospital), or when they feel daring (as when teenagers are out on a Friday night), or when inattentive people do not bother to stop (as when people allow driving to take second place to their conversation or date).

However true these practical points are, for the person who is concerned with living a decent, ethical life, the question must be not just how people do act, but how people ought to act. Exploring political obligation challenges us to think about how we ought to act toward our political system. It calls on us to think as ethical people. Moreover, the experience of recent years, as in the past, suggests that we never know when we will be impelled by circumstance, or by conscience, to have to answer in life the ancient questions: Am I obligated? Are we obligated? Should I obey? Should we obey?

SUGGESTIONS FOR SUPPLEMENTARY READING

Brecht, B. *The Measures Taken*. In *The Jewish Wife and Other Short Plays*. New York: Grove Press, 1965.

Burke, Edmund. *Reflections on the Revolution in France*. Indianapolis: Library of Liberal Arts, 1955.

Camus, Albert. *The Rebel*. New York: Vintage, 1956.

Lenin, V. I. *What Is To Be Done?* New York: International Publishers, 1929.

Locke, John. *The Second Treatise on Government*. Many editions.

Nomad, M. *Apostles of Revolution*. New York: Collier, 1961.

Pitkin, Hannah. "Obligation and Consent II." *American Political Science Review* (March 1966): 39–52.

Socrates (Plato). *Apology* and *Crito*. Many editions.

Sophocles. *Antigone*. Many editions.

Walzer, Michael. *Obligations*. Cambridge, Mass.: Harvard University Press, 1970.

Wolff, Robert Paul. *In Defense of Anarchism*. New York: Harper & Row, 1970.

8
Authority and Revolt

We are, as Aristotle observed almost 25 centuries ago, "political animals." We inherit our interdependence, and the benefits of social interactions that we experience draw us toward political communities, in spite of the risks and inconveniences that they inevitably bring. We accept crowded conditions and submit to unpleasant restrictions of individual liberty in order to share in such benefits as the provision for common welfare and increased opportunities for achievement that political communities provide. As typical political animals who share the same territory at the same time in history, we must balance our dependence and independence. Consequently, each of us has a significant, unavoidable stake in our social and political structures.

To be sure, we have a taste and a tolerance for remarkable variety in political and social arrangements. History bears witness to a range of political communities, from tightly organized, tiny nomadic clans to loosely integrated superstates, from simple oral arrangements to reams of fine-print regulations, from an oligarchy of a few elders to monolithic bureaus, with every conceivable arrangement in between. There are those who advocate a single political community of mankind—a concept that seems less ridiculous now, because global communications are a reality. This diversity of institutions is ample evidence of our search for a viable polity. For example, anarchists who reject states as we know them and statists who embrace them may disagree about what a desirable political community is, but they agree that the necessity exists to relate to each other, to accommodate our differences, and to make the most of our potentials. The dispute between them and most of us centers not on the end but on the means—on how complex or simple, arbitrary or permissive, the community's institutions should be. Similarly, those who rely on divine guidance and those who do not, agree on at least one point: The desire for political organization is a human characteristic. They may disagree about its origins and purposes just as much as the Ayatollah Khomeini's supporters and the Shah's supporters did, but there is consensus on the need for human beings to have polities in order to relate to each other in the public sector.

This simple truth raises an important issue, however. If we accept states and their institutions as being permanent human phenomena, then questions about authority and revolt become critically important. In the twentieth century the locus of politics is overwhelmingly in the nation-state. But wherever the locus, we are faced with the task of establishing a polity that furthers our aspirations and permits us to move beyond the bare rudiments of individual survival. Authority and revolt become significant factors in the establishment of desirable political communities, because even the most desirable political relationships lack permanence. And often our best efforts achieve something far less than the political ideal. We place great value on our polities, because we need them. When they satisfy our desires and needs, we become complacent and bask in our good fortune. We do not see the need for prudent evaluation. But when states go awry, we feel a keen sense of shock and emptiness and a panicky need to find viable alternatives.

LOYALISTS AND REBELS

Political institutions that mock justice and pervert moral values are far from rare. Even the most casual student of history knows about the terrors of the Stalinist dictatorship, the horror and depravity of the Third Reich, the chilling stories that filter out of the "banana republic" military juntas with their death squads, and other instances of the suffering and enslavement that people experience too often, regardless of time and place. Even in the United States the extremely poor, especially the rural and ghetto blacks, sometimes feel the arbitrary baton of the angry police officer and experience deprivation of civil liberties or incarceration, resulting from the inadequacies of a system that forces people accused of crimes to languish in frightful prisons. The proponents of the so-far unratified Equal Rights Amendment to the U.S. Constitution, for example, point out that women have suffered serious economic and social—if not political—discrimination, even in the relatively progressive U.S. polity. We may be shocked to discover that the government we have come to depend on and believe in has, in some instances, changed from one of protection to one of persecution. Even if we are not affected personally, we can see less fortunate citizens denied the benefits of freedom and justice in a system that professes to guarantee both.

When polities pervert justice, not only do the directly affected victims suffer, but those who have come to view political institutions as being public spirited become disillusioned. We do not want chaos and unfulfilled opportunities, and the disappearance of formerly dependable stability is chaotic and unfulfilling. This is why we approach questions about the relative merits of our state and the possibility of revolt with great reluctance, if at all. Yet, we must question our politices all of the time. To face an issue suddenly and without preparation is far worse than to face it armed with the knowledge and understanding that comes only from careful political thinking in calm and reflective times.

Revolt cannot be logically separated from the political relationships within a state, the denial of justice, the abuse of authority, and individual and collective political obligations. Before individuals elect to seek redress through rebellion or to accept bad conditions complacently, they should decide whether the state has legitimate authority and therefore deserves their obedience and loyalty, or whether the state has abused authority entrusted to it. If a polity is legitimate—that is, if its authority does not stem from a tyrannical abuse of power and serves moral ends—individual decisions may not be difficult. Life is usually not easy, however. If the polity is only partially representative, or if it is wholly tyrannical, people are confronted with a very difficult task. They must construct a thoughtful base for action, built on judgment and argument about fundamental questions of political morality.

The misuse of authority and the rebellion it creates is common and affects individuals and governments, regardless of time and place. In the comparatively short history of the United States, citizens have had to choose between armed rebellion and loyalty to England, between following Danial Shays in his armed rebellion against the government and accepting unfulfilled promises to the common farmers, between slavery and freedom for blacks, between Northern or Southern forces in the Civil War, between support for American involvement in the war with Mexico and the disobedience Thoreau encouraged, between gunboat diplomacy by which we seized the Panama Canal and opposition to unlawful acquisition, and between support for territorial expansion in the seizure of the Philippines and peaceful coexistence with China, among other issues.

Nor has our own era escaped crises of authority and rebellion. The Vietnam War and the opposition and resistance to governmental regulations it prompted is a recent example. So is our support of repressive dictatorships in Latin countries and elsewhere. There are still, even now, Americans in foreign countries whose protest of the Vietnam War led to their voluntary exile and who have not changed in their adamant rejection of American policies and authority. The headlines report the rebellion of those who oppose continued American nuclear arms buildups, sometimes using peaceful means and sometimes violence. The Amish and some evangelical Christians who object to compulsory public education on religious grounds wage a continuing battle with public school officials in several states, and many who allow their children to go to public schools demand control over the content of textbooks and curricula for all, not merely their own children. Many blacks in the United States feel that they have been victims of discrimination for centuries and that they owe nothing to the country that perpetuated the inequalities. Ghetto riots in the 1960s appeared sometimes to be open, if inchoate, rebellion, and they still flare from time to time, as Miami saw in the early 1980s.

The members of the Committee to Reelect the President who were involved in the Watergate scandals admitted that many acts Richard Nixon ordered them to perform were illegal or immoral. Were their actions justified on the grounds of national security? Were they morally committed to continue to be loyal to the authority that originally justified their acts or to rebel against it? Was the "debategate" scandal of Reagan's people stealing the Carter briefing papers for the 1980 presidential debate a similar matter to those involved? Daniel Ellsberg, the defense analyst who originally supported U.S. Vietnam War policy, but changed after seeing classified documents detailing our policies and atrocious tactics, was placed in a similar dilemma. Was he obligated to continue to support the authority he had sworn loyalty to? Was his decision to disassociate himself from that authority in the name of patriotism justified? Should he have given those documents to the *New York Times?* Should the *Times* and the *Washington Post* have rebelled against the authority of the state by printing what Ellsberg had given them? Should American newsmen have sneaked into Grenada to report the U.S. invasion there, when they were expressly barred from doing so by the president? People who opposed U. S. involvement in Vietnam or later involvement in Central America, but nevertheless were asked to serve in the armed forces or pay taxes to finance the war efforts, were also forced to make a choice. What should they have done? What should women who are not guaranteed equal pay for equal work do? Those people of moderate means who are asked to make substantial economic or personal sacrifices in a government fiscal crisis, while they read daily headlines about massive tax giveaways to the rich and the large corporations and their record profits, are also faced with choices. What should they do? What about French-speaking people from Quebec facing the 1982 Canadian constitution which they felt to be highly discriminatory against them? Were they right in acquiescing to it?

No matter what our position in the polity, as these examples show, each of us is liable to be faced with hard, if subtle, choices about authority and revolt. The examples here are American, but the problems are universal. If we are confronted by situations that run counter to our morality, we should at least consider whether we ought to continue our former obligations in spite of changed circumstances, or whether we should (or must) seek to oppose injustice through revolt. We must also remember that not to decide is to make a decision. The price of political interdependence, the continuing application of moral evaluations, cannot be avoided if we want to live in political communities that benefit citizens instead of leaders.

THE MORAL DIMENSION OF REVOLT

Revolt is above all a moral subject that political theory can address. The moral dimensions of authority and revolt demand careful analysis, because they are an integral part of responsible citizenship. This analysis is based on our theories of political obligation and the values that support them. In fact, the whole process of thinking about authority and revolt can best be viewed as a logical progression from the understanding of political obligation to prescriptions about the ends and means of revolt.

Like all political theory, thinking about obligation begins from a basic political value. Usually this value is some variation on the theme of the sanctity of life, although any other value is possible. Other norms often valued and defended include liberty, equality, justice, and participation. On the basis of these values, it is axiomatic to this approach to revolt that we ought to be obligated to political communities that make such values secure—and that we cannot be obligated to polities that do not.

A theory of political obligation is a sword with two sharp edges. In the delineation of a set of values and policies embodied in a good polity, an obligation theory functions as a standard by which to measure the appropriateness of our loyalty to that polity. For example, if our theory of obligation justifies obligation only to a state that maximizes the general welfare of the community, while it protects specified individual rights of each citizen, we have a clear definition of the aims of a legitimate political authority. If we then apply this concept to a particular state and find that the polity in question fails to measure up to its obligation to its citizens, are we obligated to it? Of course not. Its claims on our loyalties depend on its discharge of its obligation. Our specifications of what is right tell us that this particular political community is immoral. In addition, it gives us a set of standards to determine how immoral it is—we can perceive the distance between specifications and performance and thereby determine the seriousness of the situation. Continuation of even our once-justified obligation in this circumstance would mock our values and commit us to immorality. Thus, our theory of what is right (the first edge of the sword) also tells us which states we are morally obligated to support and which ones we should not follow (the second edge), as well as giving us a measure of relative state immoralities. We must use both of these edges in cutting through the thicket of questions of authority and revolt in order to reach a morally defensible position. When we put our values to work in this way, we discover the degree of legitimacy in our political communities and open up to view a great many alternatives of justifiable citizen behavior.

Although the process of political thinking described here appears to be simple, the application of the process is often quite complex. For one thing, political systems cannot be neatly segregated into absolutes of black and white, good and evil. We often have difficulty in identifying many of the factors that we must consider for the assessment of a complex political community. Even when we are able to identify general trends and much specific detail, our assessment depends on how our values fare in the present, how they have evolved historically, and their most likely survival in the future. There is no available guaranteed formula to apply. Critical judgment must always be exercised in such important determinations, and that requires understanding, reflection, and rational evaluation. That, of course, is the major goal of systematic political theory.

We all know, however, that the times when the calm voice of reason is needed most are often those when it eludes us. Tyranny and social upheaval carry us to the brink and often over the precipice of crisis, clouding dispassionate and reasonable assessment of events, inflaming emotions and fears, arousing our narrow self-interest, and blinding us to the possible conflict of our acts with our ultimate political values. Thucydides, for example, was deeply involved in Athenian policy making during the time when the critical decisions to enter the Peloponnesian War were being made;[1] his position on the question of whether Athenian imperialism was wrong and whether to maintain his loyalties to her after a long exile and disgrace was surely influenced by his personal interests in the situation. Or, consider the case of Sir Thomas More who had to choose between his obligations to his king and to his church on the question of sanctioning a royal divorce.[2] Was his refusal to obey royal orders, emanating from a monarch who was likely to get his way in any event, worth More's head? In this case, revolt can certainly be judged to have been futile, though not obviously foolish. Yet, More's devotion to the church and his stubbornness in time of crisis did not allow him to make a rational assessment; he never seriously considered any path other than the one to the executioner, even though the options were there.

Even when we find it difficult, we must try to follow a reasoned progression from basic political values to decisions about revolt. We cannot eschew this reasoned progression, if we want to maintain polities that enhance the prospects of just political accommodation, instead of uneasy coexistence built on mutual suspicion. Turbulent times, above all others, demand thoughtful ethical concern, if we are to avoid nihilism and irrationalism when their lure is greatest. We may not always succeed but we must make the attempt, if our political obligations and values are not to be merely hollow words recited on patriotic occasions. The consequences of failure in a nuclear age demand more than ever that we make a heroic effort to succeed.

Since political communities vary widely in their worth, our first task is to decide which deserve our political obligation and which do not. When we find that a given polity is one that is consistent with our values and therefore is, in our judgment authoritative, we have only to determine an appropriate way to fulfill our obligations. But when we cannot obligate ourselves to a particular polity because it offends our values, we must find the most appropriate avenues of opposition to it, in order to give meaning to our values.

In this latter instance, we face two critical questions: What levels of political opposition are required, and what means may we use to pursue them? The answers to these questions depend primarily on our personal values and the personal risks we are willing to take. These two questions are recurrent. No citizen has complete immunity to issues of authority and revolt. An analysis of some of the more important theories dealing with these issues can prepare us for their sudden or gradual intrusion into our personal world. Political theory can supply us with some guidelines that can lessen the impact of such emergencies on our lives.

PROVISIONAL OBLIGATION

As we start our analysis of the continuum of behaviors available to citizens, the most conservative position that is morally defensible is provisional obligation—being obligated to a political community, provided that it meets our criteria of a good polity. As we shall detail below, it commits us to the pursuit of important values without mindlessly tying ourselves to a given polity, irrespective of what it does. Since our obligation is provisional, the right to reject that obligation, if the polity no longer deserves it, is intrinsic to provisional obligation.

Most citizens are satisfied, or at least not actively dissatisfied, with their states. This may be due only to their low levels of expectation that arise from past deprivations and the political socialization process, in which family, schools, churches, media, peer groups, and the like often work in concert to reinforce satisfaction with public institutions (whether deserved or not) that at the same time encourage only limited involvement. Or it may be due to the fact that a good many states plod along doing a minimally satisfactory, if unspectacular, job of administration in the area of many public needs.[3] Whatever the cause, surveys show that in most polities, including our own, a majority of the people accept their institutions, though they are often apathetic toward them.

Citizens who live in a state that is good, or as is often the case, one that they perceive to be good, are fortunate because they face no great moral crisis. It is easy to accept obligation when the state accomplishes what one values. The only real problem, then, is to discover how to discharge their moral obligations in an appropriate way. Thus, even though such citizens need not actively concern themselves with revolt, they must still ask themselves what duties their obligations entail. Also, since their obligations are rooted in their values, as well as in the actual performance of the government itself, they must realize the inherently tenuous nature of obligation to a specific political community.

The question of what constitutes morally appropriate modes of obligation has been answered by a great many political thinkers. Furthermore, policy makers, who are not often great political thinkers, deluge us with their ideas of the valid civic duties of obligated citizens. For example, a form of the benefit theory of obligation advanced by many governments (including the United States) claims that we must serve in the military if drafted, because we have benefited from the advantages of citizenship and, therefore, have certain obligations to the state—determined exclusively by the state. We agree that the benefit theory of obligation is persuasive,[4] but the form in which this obligation to the state should be fulfilled must respond to the individual as well as the state. People often have multiple obligations—to ideals, families, or jobs, as well as to the state—obligations that are, by definition, morally weighted. A state, like an individual, must acknowledge the complex moral debts and responsibilities most adults have, just as an individual who has benefited from the state must not seek to escape his resultant obligation.

Some citizens refuse to participate in wars, for example, even if they have an obligation to the state, claiming they have a higher obligation to moral laws against war. Some governments, on the other hand, often ignore citizens' multiple obligations, including pacifistic ones, and demand that everyone actively support a war. Neither position is very convincing. The provisions for alternative service represent a very positive step that some societies, including our own, have taken to avoid such dilemmas in the real world in which people have multiple obligations. In this case, alternative service offers a way for citizens to acknowledge their obligations both to higher law and to the state. Our only quibble with it in our society is that its requirements are too narrowly drawn.

We may well owe a good political community a great deal, but since a political community is good only insofar as it serves the interests of its members, its calls to duty must harmonize, as much as is humanly possible, with the other obligations and values citizens have. Polities can do much in this regard, and perhaps we may reject a claim to duty to even the best of states, if the only rationale for such a claim is official endorsement that rests on a limited view of the public interest.

If we look to the history of political theory for guidance, we see that the ancient Greeks delineated a group of civic responsibilities that remain sensible in our age.[5] They argued that obligated citizens ought to participate in all of the civic decisions, duties, and opportunities, including paying their fair share of the cost of public facilities provided to them by the constitution and customs of their polity. They ought to be informed about the issues of the day, honor the best interests of their fellow citizens, and take advantage of the full rights of citizenship accruing to people in their particular polity.

The validity of such a view can be best illustrated by comparison with the prescriptions of the medieval theorist St. Augustine. He felt that temporal communities exist only as way stations before eternity. The sinful nature of unsaved individuals causes nations to be hotbeds of greed and depravity. The temporal communities exist to save people from themselves and give them a chance at eternal salvation. The civic duties owed such a polity include unquestioned obedience, irrespective of individual citizens' values. The obligation is owed to God through the polity, and if the state says to die for it, the good citizen must do so, because God wills only justice in the long run.

Many theologians and political theorists, from Aquinas to Niebuhr, have rejected at least the political aspects of these claims. While not denying divine authority, they have claimed that the political community is a human one and consequently must be organized around human values and needs. A modern adaptation of the classical Greek position is on the right track. Thus, those whose idea of a good polity has been met by their state owe to it behavior that will continue to make it good for them and their fellow citizens. Their civic participation will tend to keep the polity consistent with what caused it to become the accepted authority in the first place. Therefore, the polity cannot violate their political values if they and their fellow citizens act in this way.

While we may quibble with the specific application of the Greek theory, it does make sense that the fulfillment of the aspirations of its citizens is what makes a state authoritative. Citizens should do what is expected of them, exercise full legal rights, and advocate constitutional change, as long as their values are not being violated by the state.

The test issue of political obligation often arises when the state asks citizens to give their lives. The seventeenth-century English thinker Hobbes and the eighteenth-century Swiss thinker Rousseau exemplify two classic opposing views on the obligation to die for the state as the ultimate civic duty.[6] Hobbes felt that the state ought to exist only as an instrument designed to fulfill the right of self-preservation for each of its citizens. No one was ever obligated to die for it.[7] On the other hand, Rousseau felt that the polity was so much a beneficial aspect of the common life of its citizens that it was proper to expect a citizen to risk death for it, so that the benefits of the political community would be preserved for others.[8]

While fairness to Rousseau demands that we point out that he meant this only for politics that were radically egalitarian and democratic (as he envisioned in his *Social Contract*), the issue between Rousseau and Hobbes, apart from their particular formulations, remains a basic one. For those who view provisional obligation favorably, Hobbes's argument will seem most convincing. His insistence that the sanctity of life is a fundamental political value will not be discredited by any arguments for the organic unity of a political community or any other collectivist arguments of ultrapatriotic people who do not recognize the individually based needs polities must serve. To the provisionally obligated, no state can expect its members to violate their most cherished values (their right to existence) simply because it has provided them with other valued things, such as good relationships between fellow citizens in the public arena. The most positive benefits of a good public life are derived from life's continuance for each and every citizen.

Advocates of provisional obligation insist that the duties owed to a good state are proportional to its inclusion of humanistic values that are the basis of our theories of obligation. In the final analysis, we are obligated to other citizens through our political communities. Institutions are not thinking entities and cannot enter into moral relationships, such as obligation. An institution is authoritative only insofar as it is governed by our political values. This being the case, wise citizens should view their obligatory civic duties to the beneficiary political community through a lens of constant moral reevaluation. They are provisional upon being deserved. Good states do go awry, and we should attempt to prevent that possibility by viewing the actions of even the best states in a mildly skeptical manner. To do otherwise is folly, because an unprovisional pledge of civic duty without a guarantee of our values is a mindless act of automatic obedience, not the thinking act of a sophisticated citizen. The surest way to guarantee the existence of authoritative political communities is to populate them with authoritative citizens who will ask hard questions about the benefits of government. Their loyalty can be earned, but it is not automatic—it is provisional on being deserved.

Provisional obligation, though a conservative position, is an attractive one. It is an act of value application characterized by moral and rational behavior, instead of merely reflexive acts usually associated with patriotism for its own sake. To be sure, political communities are valuable[9] and they should be given the benefit of the doubt on questions of authority. They ought not to be disposed of on a whim or in a momentary passion inflamed by some exciting issue. It presumes that a state that fulfills the valid moral objectives that constitute its being should be obeyed, and asks only that the forms of civic duty associated with obedience be consistent with the moral rationale for the state.

Moreover, in its requirement for constant reassessment, provisional obligation gives clear criteria for the specific bases of a political community's authoritativeness. It places the requirement of moral evaluation and active citizenship on the ordinary person, but it gives fair value for the price exacted: It improves the prospects of a good polity by providing direction for other actions when the polity is less than good. The entire idea of social-contract theory in Western history (in the political theories of Hobbes, Rousseau, Locke, Jefferson, and others) is intimately associated with such a view of provisional obligation. While the various social-contract theorists do not agree on the exact nature and limits of the civic duties expected, their agreement that moral public institutions and behavior should provisionally obligate the citizen is impressive, and is sufficient cause for us to take this particular theory of authority and revolt seriously.

PARTIAL OBLIGATION

When most of a polity's institutions, laws, and policies are morally valid and deserve obligation, but some particular ones are not, citizens are in a dilemma. They are morally obligated to those aspects of the community that are good. Hence, they cannot simply reject the polity and work for its overthrow. They should not, however, tolerate its evil aspects. In such a situation, they have no choice but to be simultaneously loyal citizens and sworn enemies of selected aspects of their political community—partially obligated and partially rebellious. They must be loyal to that which is morally valid. They must oppose and work to change that which is immoral—that which they cannot condone. Their civic duty is to act loyally to the extent that the polity merits it and not when it does not fulfill basic, reasonable standards for political obligation.

THE QUESTION OF CIVIL DISOBEDIENCE

While people seek by many means to change society to accord more adequately with their norms, none is more controversial or raises more important questions in political philosophy, except for revolution, than acts of civil disobedience. Civil disobedience may be defined as any purposeful, public act of disobedience to any polity, institution, or law. It is usually employed by those who consider themselves partially obligated, only after more conventional and legal means of change have been exhausted. It is particularly suited to the dilemma of the partially obligated. Civil disobedients follow this route rather than revolution, because they seek to improve rather than overturn the society, and they do not deny its adequacy or even desirability in many areas. To advocate revolution is to declare war on a political community and to deny its authority altogether.

Civil disobedience has several important characteristics. First, it is an act of what Walzer terms the "morally serious" citizen.[10] It is not the criminal act of a thief, carried out in his own self-interest, and without valid claims of political morality legitimately associated with it. Civil disobedients act in a public—a political—manner that is designed to educate their fellow citizens about a moral crisis. They try to point out a wrong by their opposition and to cause people in and out of the policy process to become concerned enough to put a halt to the outrage. Far from doing something in their own interest and hoping to slink away and escape detection and punishment like thieves or terrorists, people acting on the basis of political morality commit an act in full public view with the clear intention of being caught and tried, so that their prosecution can be viewed publicly as persecution and stand as an example of moral bankruptcy. They schedule their act so that it can be seen and understood by the largest audience and to ensure that they will be apprehended. Some even go so far as to alert the news media and the police beforehand. There is no private benefit in being arrested, incarcerated, and risking the prospect of severe punishment. No jewels are stolen, no banks robbed (even to pay for other activities of a political nature), and no fortunes made by civil disobedients. Their only victims are immoral policies.

Acts of civil disobedience have occurred frequently in American history, including many by those we celebrate as great patriots. A few examples may illustrate the political and moral character of the act. Perhaps the most famous incident of civil disobedience in our history was the Boston Tea Party, in which a group of colonists threw a cargo of British tea into Boston Harbor to protest the taxation the British had levied against Americans without giving them representation in the government that passed the levy. This was a classic example of accepting overall British authority. (It was not an act of rebellion—that was to come later.)

It followed our definition in every way except that the participants tried to hide their identities to escape British wrath, although they communicated by public notices who they were in general and why they had acted. The moral significance of their act would have been enhanced if, as a demonstration of the colonists' will to resist, they had allowed the British to capture them. Nevertheless, it was civil disobedience.

In recent years conscientious resistance to the draft or even registration for a possible future draft for military service has also been civil disobedience. Many young men when called refused to register or to take the oath of induction, or publicly destroyed or returned their registration cards, to protest conscription policies that they felt were immoral. Many willingly went to jail rather than into the army. Those who fled to Canada and elsewhere in the Vietnam era rejected the whole polity and did not commit civil disobedience. The ones, however, who stayed, refused, and willingly took their punishment were operating entirely within the boundaries of civil disobedience. Similarly, the act of Daniel Ellsberg, who made public classified documents detailing the nature of American foreign policy in Southeast Asia, and the defiant willingness of the editorial staffs of the *New York Times* and the *Washington Post* (and later other newspapers) to print the material given to them by Ellsberg, in order to expose the nature of American actions and produce public outrage at these policies, fall within the realm of civil disobedience, as well. There have been countless other acts by Americans in the past and present, ranging from the antiwar efforts of various Quaker protesters to mass antibusing protests. The recent blockading of the Seneca Army Depot in New York by anti-nuclear-weapons activists, and the attempt by similarly inclined British activists in the 1980s to prevent the deployment of U.S. nuclear-tipped cruise missiles at Greenham Commons also follow the trend.

Conscientious lawbreakers affirm the authoritative nature of their political communities by their choice of civil disobedience, rather than more sweeping protests such as revolution. They communicate the idea that the state has a right to have institutions and policies, to pass laws and to punish violators, by their willingness to be caught and accept punishment for their acts, if their legal and political defenses fail. They demonstrate their political obligations by caring enough about public policies to be concerned about their effect on others. They believe that people need political communities to relate effectively to each other. They show a desire not to destroy the polity and a passion to improve it. Thus, any act that is really civil disobedience must be without intentional private gain, must be open, and must be clearly justified through communication of its moral rationale. Moreover, it must be limited. The aim is to improve the state by purging it of evil. Therefore, the disobedient eschews the moral outlook and the tactics of the revolutionary and of the totally obedient simultaneously. His is a difficult middle ground of moral seriousness buttressed by political obligation.

Some thinkers like Hugo Bedeau have maintained that civil disobedience must be nonviolent in order to fall short of revolution.[11] Such claims are understandable, because they focus on the inherently limited nature of civil disobedience. As a practical matter, however, the absence or presence of violence is not relevant as a factor of the definition of civil disobedience.

There are several considerations with regard to violence and civil disobedience that should be looked at, because the issue is so important. First of all, one must be careful about the word violence. While it is normally understood as the use of force to injure or abuse, we must distinguish between violence directed at bricks, mortar, and wood—that is, violence against property—and violence directed at people. There is a great deal less suffering caused by violence against property than there is in violence against flesh and blood. The latter is more serious and more deserving of moral condemnation. An act of civil disobedience that encompasses violence should be as limited in that respect as possible and clearly likely to lower violence in the long run (such as violently destroying a band of state-sanctioned terrorists and thereby preventing them from killing thousands), if it is to be defensible on moral grounds.

Second, it should be understood that practitioners of civil disobedience do not agree on the relative pragmatic merits of violence. Violence is often thought to be more effective, all other things being equal, because pacific sentiments are felt to "be in the way" and "petty moralisms" have no place in the tactics of those who stand up courageously against injustice. This rationale for violent civil disobedience is of dubious merit. Careful planning and intelligence can make nonviolent actions tremendously effective, as was the recent blockade of key Alpine passes by French truckers protesting President Mitterand's policies. Violence is often thought of as the last resort of the incompetent. Those who feel that they ought to use it without hesitation are often guilty of poor tactical as well as moral vision.

Frankly, much of the violence in civil disobedience is preventable by better planning and intelligence and, in any case, tactical considerations should take a back seat to moral considerations in an act that is predicated on public morality. If some violence is absolutely necessary however (as in the case of destroying the terrorists), if something is to be prevented that would be much worse, the best principle to pursue is that of an economy of violence. Civil disobedients who wish to give prominence to moral considerations should use the least violent tactics available to them and should reject any acts that would be extremely violent, regardless of their intended consequences. There is a point, indeed, where what one does in the service of morality is so monstrous that it can never make up for what it would prevent. The civil disobedient must never reach that point, and this is what gives at least partial credibility to those who condemn violence in civil disobedience. Unavoidable violence in civil disobedience must always be held to the absolute minimum. It is always regrettable and should never be celebrated.

Any evaluation of the moral appropriateness of civil disobedience has to take two major positions into account. The first, held by such theorists as Bay and Thoreau,[12] claims that states will always tend toward injustice unless they are curbed by justice-loving citizens. People who wish to see their political communities maintain morality, therefore, constantly need to check government, and in extreme cases, this may require civil disobedience. The claim is not that political institutions are evil and can do no good, but that large institutions tend to lose sight of their goals and need occasional rude shocks to nudge them into regaining their original vision. When necessary, civil disobedience can supply such shocks, and perhaps at times civil disobedients should be viewed as the most loyal of citizens. Perhaps they are if they act out of a desire to see their polities live up to their promise and improve the quality of public life.

On the other hand, we must recognize the case against civil disobedience. Many thinkers, like Augustine or Burke,[13] opposed civil disobedience. They put a great deal more faith in the polity's intrinsic justice without assistance. Augustine believed that the state acts in concert with God's plan, and Burke held that it developed its policies and institutions through the arduous trials and errors of history and, therefore, was not likely to lose sight of its purposes or to serve injustice. Others worry that acts of disobedience are likely to be dangerous, because public order is so fragile. Civil disobedience, they fear, might destroy the whole fabric of the community, and thus the risks are not worth running. To tamper with what we dimly understand is to risk the unleashing of dark forces that may engulf us all before they are contained.

This latter position is not entirely implausible, because of the effects of fads and mob behavior in societies. On the other hand, even the best-conceived and best-administered of polities sometimes loses touch with the needs of its citizens, due to the isolation of its leaders and the cultural lag intrinsic to institutions. It is not anarchic to reserve the right (some would take it even farther and make it a duty) to rerail polities when they jump the track of justice. Augustine and Burke simply place too much faith in political institutions in the real world of human experience. It is not realistic to expect them to stay on the track, no matter what happens. We agree that states are valuable and should not be resisted capriciously, but we cannot concur in the claim that good reasons never exist for resistance or that limited resistance always leads to ruin. Also, it is obvious that it should never be undertaken lightly or without awareness of unwanted consequences. In fact, however, it may often prevent, rather than ensure, the ruin of a political society. There are times when a course of civil disobedience is in the long-range self-interest of those who seek the best possible political communities, however distasteful it might be to the ordinary citizen who is unaccustomed to even partial nonobligation. The short-run tactical risks and inconveniences that civil disobedience might cause should be balanced against the long-range gains it often accomplishes.

In trying to assess civil disobedience we must conclude that it can be a legitimate and justifiable response of those citizens whose theory of political obligation tells them to maintain their general political loyalties, even when selected aspects of their polities are wrong and are beyond legal recourses for change. On a purely practical level, civil disobedience will succeed only when the state and its citizens have at least a residue of moral concern. If you had tried to lie down in front of Hitler's tanks in order to halt them, your act would have been futile. It would have been swiftly nullified when you were run over and killed. Nevertheless, purely practical considerations should never take precedence in moral definition and analysis in political theory. An act of morally serious civil disobedience is a valid one, regardless of whether its intended consequences are fulfilled. Citizens who feel that their obligations command them to save the polity, instead of rejecting it, should consider civil disobedience as a valid alternative at their command.

STATES WITHOUT AUTHORITY: ENDS, MEANS, AND MORALITY IN THE OBLIGATION TO DISOBEY

There is a line, not always obvious, between legitimate and illegitimate political communities. Thinkers who judge their communities worthy of obligation are obviously dealing with polities that are on the "good" side of that line. Civil disobedients, on the other hand, are frequently working with communities that straddle the line. There is surely a great deal of good in their communities, or they would not feel that such polities are worth saving. Some political communities, however, have crossed the line. They are not morally justifiable. Such unauthoritative states have gone too far down the road to tyranny to be worthy of redemption. These are the kinds of communities that rebels attack.

Potential rebels have only their theories of obligation to guide them. They know what legitimate authority is; they know that they are not experiencing it. Beyond this, what are they to think? What issues will they have to consider? The first question is, Why should they rebel? What tactics ought to be used? The question of what justifies revolution will be analyzed at some length below. The second question is equally vexing and not easily answered.

First, then, we must ask why revolution is ever justified. We believe that no one need support an unjust state, but are there good grounds for actively opposing one? After all, revolution is a step fraught with serious moral and practical consequences. Almost all thinkers on revolution in the modern era agree that revolutionary opposition of one sort or another finds it legitimate justification in opposition to human oppression or injustice. They also tend to agree that this step must always be a final, desperate action, taken only when all other means of redress have been exhausted. They usually insist as well that oppression and injustice must be grievous and enduring in their impact. Revolutions must not be undertaken for light causes. They can cost too much in human life and suffering.

Where agreement ends, however, is over what constitutes oppression or injustice and over who may determine when they exist. Thoreau is renowned for his declaration that it is up to everyone, individually to decide when government is doing great human evil and when revolt is justified. Others have shared this anarchical notion, but it is a position that should be viewed skeptically. There is always a reason to wonder if any individual, or even a minority group, can be so certain of its grievances as to give it a moral right to plunge a society into the dangers and destruction of revolution. Others warn that such individuals, if they are moved by genuine moral concern, must ask what a good society does for others, for the majority. Individuals should hesitate before they dismiss the benefits a society may provide for others. If they exist, they cannot justify oppression, but they do weaken the case for revolution.

These considerations, among others, moved John Locke as well as many democrats to insist that a revolution cannot be legitimate unless a majority believes it is, unless a majority believes that the grievances and injustices in society are too great. They make majority opinion the criterion of human oppression. They argue, as all democrats must, that government is properly founded in the consent of the governed. Only a majority may withdraw consent and justify a revolt. Otherwise, revolution may actually lead to a minority seizing power for its selfish interests in the name of its selfish notions of oppression.

A third common basis for revolution insists that the test of human oppression must not be solely up to individuals or majorities, but recognized natural standards or rights. Violations of such alleged rights as the right to national self-determination, to political liberty, to equal political participation, or to equal fulfillment of basic needs are often used as standards of oppression and injustice. The least controversial of them is the right to life itself. Certainly, when citizens, whether a majority or a minority, find their very existence jeopardized by political institutions, it is hard to argue that they do not have a natural right to revolt. Of course, a society may decide it is necessary to proceed against these citizens anyway, but the point is that citizens may well have the right to resist actively. Hobbes went so far as to claim that a state that murders citizens is not a state at all, because governments exist in the first place to provide protection for their citizens.

Another frequently cited natural right that is alleged to justify modern revolutions is the right to national self-determination. Indeed, no other rallying cry has spurred more revolutionary action in the past 40 years. Country after country has been born in Africa and Asia under the banner of that right, even when liberation forces were already at work, as in the former British colonies in Africa. Their invariable argument is that it was immoral for Britain, or France, or Portugal, or the Netherlands to deny indigenous peoples the right to govern themselves. Today, this cry is heard in Afghanistan, from Palestinian guerillas and from the rebels of Northern Ireland. It seems to be endlessly popular. While there is nothing wrong about it, per se, it is worth noting that what is of key moral worth is the kind of government brought about by these cries, as well as their national origins. While colonialism is always morally offensive, an indigenous and exploitative neocolonialism is equally offensive for the same reason: it exploits and brutalizes citizens.

A fourth basis for revolt, common in our age, is that used by Marxist revolutionaries, who appeal neither to the individual, not to the majority, nor to one or another natural right. They use history, instead, as a justification for revolution. Marxists, including the post-Vietnam War revolutionaries of

Southeast Asia and the Cubans, argue that the historical process dictates when it is appropriate for men and women to revolt in order to realize history's destiny. They make history's supposed purpose into moral justifications of the highest order.

The problems with the selection of history as a basis of revolt are similar to those posed by natural rights. In both cases it is necessary to agree in the first place that history or nature contains discernible messages. History is so notoriously murky that it is read in almost as many different ways as there are historians, amateur or professional. How can we be sure that the Marxist readings are correct? Nature and—specifically—natural rights are similarly fertile phenomena. There are a great many conflicting opinions about which natural rights exist. For example, Ayatollah Khomeini and the supporters of the shah of Iran both advanced conflicting claims in this regard. How is anyone to sort out which are valid? Also, even if history does have a central direction, or contains certain rights, we must agree that their existence requires us to give them sound moral sanction before they can justify something as serious as revolt. Nature may well teach us that life is a central value, but this does not necessarily mean that we must agree that the value is critical enough to justify revolt.

There does not appear to be any simple formula that can tell us when revolution is justified. Here, as so often, there is no substitute for the process of normative agrument and discussion in politics by thinking, informed people. We tend to think that revolution is best justified by majority sentiment, provided that it has been formed after an informed debate. Justification by this standard is likely to avoid revolutions built on individual whims or historical fantasies. Yet we recognize that majorities can err and that individuals will sometimes be morally right, whether they justify their revolt on the basis of their own judgment, history, or natural right. Majority position wins by statistical default, so to speak. If more people favor a given position, there is a better chance that they are right.

Passive Revolt

Revolution or unlimited revolt is not the only form of complete opposition to an ongoing political regime. Intensity of opposition need not be measured by the degree of active belligerence directed toward any state. One general type of unlimited opposition to a state is passive. It does nothing overtly to oppose the institutions of the political community. Passive rebels do not throw bombs or act violently in opposition to an unjust state. Instead, they "merely" withdraw any form of loyalty and civic duty from the polity. They refuse to pay taxes, to obey laws and regulations, to be conscripted, and to do anything demanded of the citizen, even if the demands might be legitimate in another context. Such a posture can be tremendously radical in its effect, to which the general strikes in twentieth-century Europe will testify. No state can endure very long when its calls to duty are met with silence by vast sectors of its population. No wars can be fought, no people exterminated. Virtually nothing can be accomplished by a state that faces significant passive opposition.

There are several varieties of passive resistance, which we have put on a continuum of likely effectiveness. This is not to say, however, that effectiveness can be equated with morality. One of the most basic types of passive revolt is emigration. It has been used recently by the masses of non-Communist refugees from South Vietnam and by fleeing anti-Soviet Afghans. People who refuse a relationship with an unjust state often simply leave it and thereby weaken its grip on the populace by denying its authority and showing others that they can follow suit. While Hobbes condemned emigration and said it was an act of cowardice that he might understand and even condone in the right circumstances, but which he could never call moral behavior,[14] we have only to recall the many heroes like De Gaulle who have gone into exile and fought from outside their homeland to see that Hobbes overstated his case by a wide margin. For those who wish to emigrate and find circumstances favorable, it is often more effective to emigrate and keep a heavy stream of criticism and moral outrage trained on the fires of tyranny than to suffer in ineffective silence within the polity. In reality, however, emigration's effects are usually blunted, because there are always enough people left behind who are willing to cooperate with—or unwilling to oppose—tyranny. Generally, emigration, even by thousands of people, has a greater impact on polities that are worthy of partial obligation than it does on consummately evil ones because in immoral states, such acts are met with callousness or repression. Emigration is not immoral, and it can be moral and effective only if particularly talented people like the writer Solzhenitsyn can accomplish their opposition only from abroad. Normally, however, emigration as an act of revolt is not so much immoral as futile.

For those who choose not to emigrate (or who are prevented from doing so), one of the options available is individual refusal to participate. This deliberate refusal of all civic duties differs from civil disobedience because it is not selective. Such rebels do not support policies, refuse conscription, will not vote, and do nothing that will aid their polity. Unfortunately, because it is not done in solidarity with others, this, too, is often a quixotic path. Individuals acting alone cannot be effective against the might of the modern state, even if their acts are morally justified. Moreover, the refusal to become involved with others similarly inclined is a desertion from the ideal of political community and human interdependence.

The most effective moral form of passive rebellion is collective refusal to participate as citizens. Through effective political organization, citizens who are united in opposition can perform such overtly passive acts as blocking government services, general strikes,[15] the organization of counterinstitutions—such as a "people's hospital" run by citizens to care for victims of the state—and many other acts that do not explicitly attack the state, but oppose it or show its bankruptcy indirectly. Gandhi's campaign of nonviolent resistance to British occupation of India is an excellent example of passive resistance. Another is seen in the activities of Lech Walesa within Solidarity, which often edged past civil disobedience in refusing to affirm the regime.

If it is well planned, collective passive resistance is powerful. The moral courage of those who lie down unarmed in front of tanks and their refusal to kill in the name of justice can be a remarkable phenomenon that can galvanize public opinion like a fire storm. But it has its price, too! The insistence on passive acts of opposition tends to put the rebels at a tactical disadvantage, because they often must react to the state's injustice and not strike preemptively with the effectiveness of violence. It requires a great deal of coordination, a great deal of patience, and generally is the most difficult way to overthrow an evil state.

Its great advantage is that it rarely traps the rebels into unfortunate tactical contradictions of their basic values. For those pacifists whose theory of political obligation is firmly based on the sanctity of human life, it is the only permissible mode of revolt. Others, like Walesa, who seek to avoid violence but do not absolutely rule it out, also prefer at least to try passive resistance first. Like civil disobedience or provisional obligation, it can be both a moral and a successful approach to revolt.

Active Revolt

Passive revolt does not exhaust the options of the potential rebel. There is always the alternative of active revolt, including activities that go beyond refusal to cooperate and take the offensive against political communities. The active revolution strikes against the institutions and the facilities of the evil state and frontally assaults the castle of sovereignty. Active rebels are revolutionaries. They use any tactics that allow them to destroy an unjust polity and erect a better one on its ruins. Their theory of obligation requires them to pursue virtue at all costs and to be intolerant of any evil state, irrespective of immediate evils they might commit in the service of ultimate truth.

The aim of revolutionaries is change—to change the very core of the institutions and basic political relationships in their society. While they should not pursue violence for its own sake, they will not let the commission of it deter them from their tasks. They should not act alone, as individual terrorists, because that would reduce their effectiveness, render their revolt impotent, and allow tyranny another victory. The tactics they embrace are inherently collective, as well as overtly active.

Revolutionaries' sweeping and total confidence in their values is responsible for their use of unlimited force in their quest for justice. This lack of a healthy skepticism and the failure to consider that they may be wrong about even their most treasured ideals may lead them toward impatience and potential moral insensitivity.

For example, there is the case of Marxist-Leninists who overthrew the government of Russia in 1917. Using the theory of Marx and Engels as a basis, Lenin and his fellow Bolsheviks felt that history was an absolute moral guide as a step toward the classless society.[16] Buoyed by these absolutes, they saw no contradiction in wholesale guillotining of thousands of real or imagined enemies of the revolution. Other contemporary examples can be found in Iran and Kampucia. Nothing and nobody can be allowed to stand in the way of a revolution when justification is absolute and self-evident. The only moral consideration is whether the revolution succeeds or fails.

There is no simple moral judgment that can be made about total revolution. For citizens who find their political community to be beyond redemption and who have a clear and compelling view of a future order of justice, revolution is a path that cannot be automatically rejected. It requires a clear sense of solidarity with fellow victims of tyranny, and it is the most effective means available to depose unauthoritative polities. Those who seek a common justice together, because they are collective victims of injustice, know full well that their obligations as political beings are to each other and to the values that they share and not to any particular regime. And, to use less than maximum efforts in opposing injustice allows tyranny a needless advantage.

Nevertheless, the example of such total revolutionaries as Lenin or Robespierre is disturbing. The excesses of terror that they permitted tarnish their revolutionary ideals and warn us of dangers that cannot be ignored.

Rebellion

There is another concept of revolt that we call rebellion instead of revolution. The twentieth-century political thinker Albert Camus best developed this idea in *The Rebel*.[17] He argues that given man's history, total revolution leads inevitably to moral excesses. It is wrong because it sanctions unleashing a potentially cataclysmic process that might turn on its initiators—an unlimited attack on all institutions and patterns of society, easily threatening the very values it was meant to affirm. Camus wanted to justify revolt, not nihilism. Camus's rebel must be careful not to sacrifice any person for the sake of a promised future, if the rebellion is to be authentically rooted in humanistic values. Justice, a concrete entity, must never be allowed to become a dim abstraction that can serve to ratify injustice.

Camus formulated this position on revolt through an analysis of historical theories of rebellion. In pointing out the dangers of these theories he modified them, so that their humanitarianism could be preserved and their dangers lessened. "Metaphysical rebellion" is the name that Camus put to one prominent concept of revolution against injustice, referring to it as "the movement by which man protests against his condition and against the whole of creation."[18] He felt that metaphysical rebels had the right impulse, but went too far. Thinkers like Nietzsche confronted the human condition and concluded that the cause of all the misery in the world was the omniscient and omnipotent God of the Judeo-Christian tradition, who, under the guise of "good," permitted men to be tortured and killed. Thus, the metaphysical rebel denounced and attacked this God as the source of all evil, and the deity of absolute justice was placed in the temple in his place. The effect of replacing one deity with another was to justify yet another kind of absolute, equally as prone to unleash chaos.

This tendency toward excess that Camus saw in metaphysical rebellion can also be seen in what he labeled historical rebellion. He traced the transformation of metaphysical rebellion to a theory consistent with the "modern" paradigms of agnosticism or atheism that dominated nineteenth-century Western philosophical thought—the efforts of the Marxists to embrace the aims and techniques of metaphysics without accepting its assumptions. In rejecting deities, they substituted a concept of "history" or "inevitable material forces" that served the same purpose in explaining and justifying and predicting the inevitability of the march of destiny to a grand cataclysm of revolution that would permanently install the "justice" of history fulfilled.

Camus's argument is that no theory of revolution by itself, no matter how it may aim to improve our political communities, is ever morally sufficient as a prescription in political theory. It is too easy to forget the ultimate purpose of revolt and to fall into a self-defeating whirlpool of senseless actions based upon rage, without values to guide them, unless there is some integral component in the theory that would prevent it. Metaphysical and historical rebellion do not contain this component. They are not justified by basic values that are clear enough to prevent their misapplication. Unfortunately, this is a likely consequence of assuming values that contain sweeping claims that are merely asserted instead of morally substantiated.

Camus did not suggest that revolutions justified in this way would automatically result in nihilism, but he argued that they are too vulnerable to such a fate and that the risk is never worth taking in the hard and tough world of revolution. Thus, he rejected both theories—metaphysical and historical rebellion—by extensively modifying them to retain their moral direction, while erecting bulwarks against their dangers. In short, by following a sound normative method in his thoughts about authority and revolt, much like the methods we analyzed in the beginning of this text, Camus avoided the dangers of revolutionary theory, while retaining its advantages.

To establish his own alternative to revolt, Camus had only to avoid the excesses of the theories he had criticized by placing within his own theory a doctrine of limits. In The Rebel, he put it this way:

> Does the end justify the means? That is possible. But what will justify the end? To that question, which historical thought leaves pending, rebellion replies: "The means."[19]

This direct confrontation of values and techniques of rebellion illustrates that no means that will assault the basic political value of life can be permitted. Events may force such actions, but moral political theory can never endorse them, even in the midst of anti-Nazi or anticolonial action, in which Camus found himself involved.

This is the context of his crucial distinction between rebellion and revolution, which we can embrace. Revolution is a total attempt to replace whole political systems. It has a strong ideology designed to usher in a completely new order to replace an unsalvageable old order. With this aim, it cannot afford to adopt any limits. It must forge a new moral order.

Rebellion is concerned with the ethical implications of living, not merely the abstraction of life. Rebels have few illusions about the future, at least in the world they know. They do not have to be philosophers, merely thinking people. Their healthy skepticism about ultimate truths and about their own omniscience helps them to maintain an outlook of humility. They are not sure enough of the absolute validity of their values and their judgment to demand that others die for them. Recognition of error cannot turn back something as permanent as death, and it cannot make amends for serious moral transgressions. Rebels cannot put aside their vision of justice while they pursue a future millennium. Because their goals seek to advance the social act of living in an imperfect world, they cannot emulate the revolutionary by using techniques that negate life in the present in the name of some future living. Therefore, their values must make a doctrine of limits an integral, virtually living part of their theory of rebellion.

Rebels must reject any means that devalue those lives they are affirming. When Camus proclaims in *The Rebel*, "Moderation, born of rebellion, can only live by rebellion. It is a perpetual conflict continually created and mastered by intelligence,"[20] he means that rebellion is something positive that is limited by equally positive considerations. Rebels who are guided by the intellect use their intelligence and their political vision in order to strive to protect people and affirm their worth. The limits proposed are not abstract "thou shalt nots." To the contrary, they are logical derivations from previous values. As one defines life in concrete terms, it becomes clear that it is the value of living, of life itself, that limits those who live it, even as it supplies them with the drive for their own liberation. This means that values must never be compromised or postponed, even by something as drastic and necessary as rebellion. Rebels reject injustice, not for its own sake but "because it perpetuates the silent hostility that separates the oppressor from the oppressed."[21] They reject it because it slays the communion and political solidarity of living. Ruled out, therefore, are such things as deceit, perpetuation of servitude, and mindless violence. All are proscribed because "life in the community is the supreme value for the rebel,"[22] and these actions are antipolitical—they seek to divide instead of to integrate.

The position of rebellion is a formidable one. We do not have to be blind advocates of Camus's political philosophy to endorse it. In its pursuit of moral consistency it substitutes the citizen's considered basic political value for the revolutionary's metaphysic and sin of commission—of employing tactics that are inconsistent with the very aims and goals of just authority and revolt. In effect, it is not a theory of revolt itself, but an improvement on the theory of revolution that comes from a critical moral analysis of the political theory of revolution. In other words, it is a practical application of the principles enunciated in this work. If examples of rebellion are hard to find in history, it is not so much because it is impossible to accomplish, but because too many people choose not to think when it really counts. The Gandhis and Camuses and Kings of the world prove that it can be done. We would be well advised to emulate them if similar circumstances confront us.

PRESCRIPTION AND PERSPECTIVES

Without a way to relate justly to others, to realize the advantages and blunt the dangers of human interdependence, citizens are lost. Thus, without it, their political lives may approach the depressing picture sketched by Hobbes in his *Leviathan*, when he described political life without a just order as "poor, nasty, solitary, brutish, and short."[23]

Luckily, Hobbes's picture need not be an accurate one for us. Authoritative political communities are within our reach. Values and obligations that recognize the individuality of each human being and allow that individuality to flourish equally for all are what are necessary to reach them. Such a humanistic, community-minded arrangement will allow all individuals to be secure in their public dealings with others. Only in such an environment can one pursue individual needs and interests without the threats or exploitation that can lead only to stifling conformity, regimentation, or worse. If political relationships can be kept on a plane that will prevent inequality and recognize that our individuality is partly the result of our relationships with others, then we can bring the idea of just political authority into reality and thereby deny the dark potentiality in Hobbes's warnings.

Citizens with such attitudes on authority and revolt are community minded, because they have uppermost in mind the need for a just politics for all citizens. In this sense, community-mindedness and individualism are complementary values in obligation. An orientation toward the community that does not forsake individual needs will lead to theories on authority and revolt that make individual dignity possible, because the orientation is nothing more than the commitment to search for social justice. The requirement is that we keep the values and theories of such an authoritative community prominent in our decisions on whether to revolt against or obey a given political community.

The importance of this principle lies in its applicability to the many theories of revolt and authority worthy of consideration. The best approach is to view the various alternatives as being on a continuum that has a definite starting point, a specific end, and contains unambiguous guides for applying appropriate courses of action to events. Our common ideal of authority compels us to seek a just political arrangement, if we are not experiencing it. Justice is our goal, and we have only to apply it consistently in means as well as ends, in spite of the difficulty of pursuing rational and moderate courses in turbulent times. Our general principle of tactics must come from the same roots as our theories of obligation. We must try the least coercive means first and escalate only if we fail. This is the only way to limit the force of our revolt. Injustice can be opposed only in the interest of all citizens; we must try not to disrupt their life-style and, more importantly, try to preserve their dignity and rights as much as possible. Human beings are too valuable to be sacrificed for ideas, however appealing.

One should weigh the advantages as well as the disadvantages of a given polity very carefully before making a decision on revolt. After all, such decisions are very nearly irrevocable in most instances. There are such things as honest mistakes or temporary lapses of judgment that have bad consequences only in the short run and can often be corrected swiftly, if complaints are effectively articulated by citizens in a constitutional, albeit vigorous, manner. There is no pressing need for revolt against such governmental failures, since they do not prove the state to be utterly corrupt, any more than there is any pressing need to acquiesce in bad policies. Even temporarily unjust institutions or immoral policies are not automatic grounds for withdrawal of political obligations. There should be a clear and continuing violation of basic political values before one declares irrevocable opposition to some of one's fellow citizens and the community they share with us. Continued obligation, of course, is not a mindless act. One still has an obligation to oppose bad policies and try to change what is wrong in the short run.

If provisional obligation cannot be justified, we can always just ignore our problems, although that would merely perpetuate them. Our best counsel is to try to work through the poliical system to improve the situation. This allows us to put our values into practice and, by improving our political environment, is also wise self-interest. The next step, if necessary, might be civil disobedience. It is frequently sufficient to get recalcitrant polities back on the right track. The shock of citizens taking great personal risks without personal benefit, other than the hope of justice, is often enough to jar even violently unjust states to their senses and to cause effective change. While its effect was not felt swiftly enough to suit many, the antiwar movement in the United States in the 1960s and 1970s was one influence that caused the government to withdraw our military forces from Vietnam and to undertake a continuing review of the whole purposes and designs of the national foreign policy, culminating in the passage of the landmark War Powers Act. Similarly, the civil rights movement accomplished much to make the U. S. polity more just. While full-scale revolution might have accomplished the same thing, it would have been a tragic case of overkill. What is more, such action would run an unnecessary risk of promoting a worse regime, once the Pandora's box of revolution was opened. The citizens who have a genuine concern for political relationships and stable and just interactions with other citizens should not leap too far too fast—civil disobedience is a next logical step. If they cannot or do not want to do that, they should carefully monitor the serious acts of civil disobedience of others to see if they have the desired effect. As long as there are many good aspects of a political community and as long as civil disobedience has at least an outside chance to reestablish authority, it is the most logical extension of sincere obligations and desire for justice.

If civil disobedience is insufficient to redeem a polity gone awry, passive resistance is the next logical step. It is morally preferable to potentially more violent forms of revolt, because the passive resister refrains from committing overt acts of violence against others. This is balanced by the fact that the mere existence of any situation of total opposition, passive or not, is likely to produce massive social displacement for citizens, not to mention the encouragement of violent reprisal by the state in its attempt to defend itself. For pacifists, whose doctrine of limits absolutely prohibits any compromise with violence, this is the most radical step they can take. Even for the nonpacifist who nevertheless tries to avoid violence, this is a good step to follow after civil disobedience fails repeatedly. We have to have some faith that it just might be effective enough to overthrow tyranny and reestablish an authoritative polity. If we are fortunate enough to have our faith justified, more violent forms of revolt are surely overkill and should not be risked until we know they cannot be avoided. Thus, it is morally safer to try passive resistance before active resistance, in the hope of minimizing coercion. Even if coercion can never be totally avoided, we must still try to hold it at arm's length as long as possible.

The final point can either be revolution or rebellion, accepting Camus's distinction between full revolt without or revolt with a doctrine of limits. Unless revolutionaries can be sure their cause is absolutely correct and unless they do not place a high value on the life and rights of all citizens, all-out revolution should be rejected always. Its cost is too high for its value. It is immoral to buy justice with the coin of injustice. Sound political values cannot be laid aside for the duration of the revolution so that we can destroy those whom we hate in order to hasten the day of justice and love. It is a moral contradiction to do so. That is why we oppose terrorists, however just their cause may be. To avoid the moral defects inherent in revolution, citizens who must overthrow a political community without merit must be themselves meritorious in their ideas and deeds. Their values can never be shunted aside, if they really respect them. Rebellion is preferable because it unites a fear of coercion with the advantages of humanism. Rebels need not hang their heads after the battle and wonder whether their accomplishments were worth the cost. They know that they always acted in a way that reflected justice in ends as well as means. Their reward lies in this world, not in the next.

In the final analysis, citizens who judge their political community to be wanting in authority know that their values and loyalties to their fellow citizens require them to avoid unnecessary violence. They should cast about with their ideas and ideals for tactics that enable them to eradicate injustice with only as much violence as is necessary to accomplish their aims and stay within moral bounds. Thus, if that is a less vehement step than rebellion, that is ideal.

Social or political change is a cataclysmic process that cannot be accomplished without great coercion, whether directly violent or more subtle but not less insidious. We must not minimize the effect on people's fortunes, safety, and even sanity that such change brings. Nevertheless, if rebels have tried to find less coercive ways to reestablish an authoritative political community and have failed, then they must push. Tyranny, too, has its costs. Rebels can be secure in the knowledge that they recognized and met their obligations and that they brought morality to immoral times. As long as they act in a morally serious fashion and keep to their doctrine of limits, their acts will always be as close as is humanly possible to an affirmation of justice and a denial of injustice.

In the end, what is required is judgment. Citizens must know what they value and why, and how to derive a theory of political obligation from that. If they have done so and must face tyranny, they will be in a position to sidestep the dim alternatives of unknowing acquiescence in injustice or blind and undirected opposition to everything. They can judge carefully even in an hour of desperation. They can make authority meaningful by affirming justice without nihilism. Above all, humanitarianism can be maintained through this process. After all, what are we, except citizens with the power to reason and love as well as hate?

NOTES

1. Thucydides, *The Peloponnesian War* (New York: Oxford University Press, 1960).

2. Robert Bolt, *A Man For All Seasons* (New York: Random House, 1962).

3. See Chapter 7 for a review of political obligation and Chapters 6 and later sections of this chapter for discussions of the nature of authority and justice as they relate to political communities.

4. See Chapter 7.

5. Thucydides, *Peloponnesian War*. See his sketch of Athenian citizenry and civic duty throughout his book, particularly when he is discussing Pericles.

6. Michael Walzer, *Obligations* (Cambridge, Mass: Harvard University Press, 1970), pp. 77-98.

7. Ibid., p. 87.

8. Ibid.

9. See the discussion of the relationship of political institutions and the need for politics in Chapter 2.

10. Walzer, *Obligations*, p. 20.

11. See, for example, Hugo Bedeau, in *Obligation and Dissent*, ed. Donald Hanson and Robert Booth Fowler (Boston: Little, Brown, 1971).

12. See Christian Bay, "Civil Disobedience: Prerequisite For Democracy in Mass Society," in *Political Theory and Social Change*, ed. David Spitz (New York: Atherton, 1967); see also Henry D. Thoreau, *On the Duty of Civil Disobedience*, reproduced in scores of anthologies and volumes of his works.

13. St. Augustine, *The City of God* in *St. Augustine: The Complete Works* (Edinburgh: Dodds, 1871–1876); or Edmund Burke, *Reflections on The Revolution in France* (Garden City, N.Y.: Dolphin, 1961).

14. Thomas Hobbes, *Leviathan* (New York: Crowell-Collier, 1962).

15. See Georges Sorel, *Reflections on Violence* (New York: Collier, 1950), for the idea of a general strike. Sorel, however, was an active and not a passive revolutionary.

16. See George Lichtheim, *Marxism*, 2d ed. (New York: Praeger, 1965).

17. Albert Camus, *The Rebel* (New York: Vintage, 1956).

18. Ibid., p. 23.

19. Ibid., p. 238.

20. Ibid.

21. Fred Wilhoite, *Beyond Nihilism* (Baton Rouge: Louisiana State University Press, 1968), pp. 82–83.

22. Camus, *The Rebel*, pp. 286–87.

23. Hobbes, *Leviathan*, Ch. 11.

SUGGESTIONS FOR SUPPLEMENTARY READING

Authority

Berlin, Isaiah. *Four Essays on Liberty*. London: Oxford University Press, 1969.

Cassirer, Ernst. *The Myth of the State*. New Haven: Yale University Press, 1946.

Dahl, Robert. *After the Revolution: Authority in the Good Society*. New Haven: Yale University Press, 1970.

Hobbes, Thomas. *Leviathan*. Many publications.

————. *De Cive*. Many publications.

Machiavelli, Niccolo. *The Prince*. Many publications.

————. *The Discourses*. Many publications.

Plato. *The Republic*. Many publications.

Rousseau, Jean Jacques. *The Social Contract*. Many publications.

Spragens, Thomas. *Understanding Political Theory*. New York: St. Martin's Press, 1976.

Thoreau, Henry David. *Slavery in Massachusetts*. Many publications.

Walzer, Michael. *Obligations*. Cambridge, Mass.: Harvard University Press, 1970.

Revolt

Berman, Marshall. *The Politics of Authenticity*. New York: Atheneum, 1970.

Brunch, et. al. *Building Feminist Theory: Essays from Quest*. New York: Longman, 1981.

Burke, Edmund. *Reflections on the Revolution in France*. Garden City, N.Y.: Dolphin, 1961.

Camus, Albert. *The Rebel*. New York: Vintage, 1956.

————. *Resistance, Rebellion and Death*. New York: Knopf, 1960.

Ginsberg, Benjamin. *The Consequences of Consent: Elections, Citizen Control and Popular Acquiescence*. Reading, Mass.: Addison-Wesley, 1982.

Hanson, D., and R. B. Fowler, *Obligation and Dissent*. Boston: Little, Brown, 1971.

Paine, Thomas. *The Rights of Man*. Garden City, NY: Dolphin, 1961.

————. *Common Sense*. Many publications.

Sorel, Georges. *Reflections on Violence*. New York: Collier, 1950.

Spitz, David, Ed. *Political Theory and Social Change*. New York: Atherton, 1967.

Thoreau, Henry David. *Civil Disobedience*. Many publications.

Index
About the Authors

Index

About the Authors

Robert Booth Fowler is Professor of Political Science, University of Wisconsin-Madison. His main areas of interest are political theory and American politics. His most recent books include *The New Engagement: Evangelical Political Thought, 1966–1976* (1983) and *Religion and Politics in the United States* (1984).

Jeffrey Robert Orenstein, Ph.D., The University of Wisconsin-Madison is Associate Professor of Political Science, Kent State University. A specialist in political theory and public policy, as well as a generalist in political science, Orenstein's most recent work was an unpublished paper on the Moral Majority as an interest group.